THE LITTLE HANDBOOK —OF— RISK

THE LITTLE HANDBOOK OF RISK

MITIGATE IT & TURN THREATS INTO OPPORTUNITIES

ROB PEACH

gatekeeper press
Where Authors are Family
Columbus, Ohio

The Little Handbook of Risk:
Mitigate it & turn threats into opportunities

Published by Gatekeeper Press
2167 Stringtown Rd, Suite 109
Columbus, OH 43123-2989
www.GatekeeperPress.com

Copyright © 2019 by Rob Peach

All rights reserved. Neither this book, nor any parts within it may be sold or reproduced in any form or by any electronic or mechanical means, including information storage and retrieval systems without permission in writing from the author. The only exception is by a reviewer, who may quote short excerpts in a review.

The cover design, interior formatting, typesetting, and editorial work for this book are entirely the product of the author. Gatekeeper Press did not participate in and is not responsible for any aspect of these elements.

ISBN (hardcover: 9781642378122
ISBN (paperback): 9781642377569
eISBN: 9781642377576

CONTENTS

ACKNOWLEDGEMENTS XIII

EXECUTIVE SUMMARY XV

KINDYNOS OR KINDA LOSSES?—
ALL ABOUT RISK 21C 1
    Periculum 1
    The Origins of Risk 2

CHAPTER 1 3
    Context of Risk 3
        Consideration 3
        E.M. Forster and Others 3
        The Czech Republic 4
        Poem 6
        The Hardest Thing of All 7
    Reputational Risk 8
    Word of Mouth Now and Henceforth—
    Digging Deeper 9
    The Phenomenon that is the Game of Cricket 11

CHAPTER 2 19
Back to Reputation 19
    Technology, Trust and Reputation 21
    Connectivity and the Threat that it Poses 23
Employee Exploitation Über Alles 24
You've Done Too Much, Much Too Young 25
Corporate Social Responsibility 2019 and Beyond 26
    Paper on CSR as Risk Management 2005 26
    Policing the Internet—Widening the Net? 28
Issues of the Day: Cryptocurrencies—
Hype or Fair Value? 29
How to Stop Amazon From Continuing to
Sell Everything and Buying All Its Competition 30
Sporting Examples 32
Politicians 33
Conservatives—The Reputation Dilemma 34
    Reputation—a little history 35

CHAPTER 3 39
Marketing Risk: IP (intellectual property) and
EQ (emotional intelligence) 39
    Distinctive Challenges 39
    Action 40
Initiation—the Creatives 41
    Risks 41
Distribution Processes 42

Outputs 43
Impact 43
Other Sectors—A Short Exploration 44
    Charities 44
Intellectual Property 46
Social Media 47
Emotional Intelligence—The Part it Plays 48

CHAPTER 4 51
Catastrophe and Insurance: Worst-Case Scenarios 51
    Catastrophe/Disaster 51
The Credit Crunch 2007-2009 52
    The Banks 52
    De-leveraging 53
    Quantitative Easing 53
Stop Press Emerging Themes and Thinking—
New Processes, New Derivatives, Better Toolkit 54
    Brand and Reputation Risk 54
    Rigorous Analysis 54
    Value at Risk (VaR) 55
Case Study—Systemic Risk (2007-2015) 57

CHAPTER 5 63
Star Talent Risk: The Exposure to their Departure 63
    Retaining Your best Talent in a Universal
    "gig economy" Environment 63

Carrot or Stick? 64
Success, Continued 66
The Stick and the Service Industry 67

CHAPTER 6 .... **69**
Virtual Staff Risks: Managing Remotely 69
Loyalty 70
Company Culture at Airbnb 71
   Implementation of Such a Dream! 72

CHAPTER 7 .... **73**
Fintech Risk and Reward: An Opportunity
like No Other 73
Introduction 75
Fintech and the GDPR Imperative—Is it Imperative? 77
Cryptocurrency—A Revolution in the Making? 77
Blockchain 78
MifID 2.0 79
The Lamfalussy Directive 80
Active versus passive Asset Management 81
Trading Online 82
PPI—The Scandal That is Payment Protection
Insurance Mis-selling 83
Annuities and Endowments 85
   Annuities 85
Do Hedgies Hedge? 86

What About Reinsurance? 87
Behavioural Economics 88

CHAPTER 8 .... **91**
The Dangers of Over-Borrowing 91
The Minsky Moment 92
Quantitative Easing (QE) 93

CHAPTER 9 .... **103**
Equity and Flotation Risks: Your other lifeline—
how to keep stakeholders happy 103

CHAPTER 10 .... **107**
Social Media/Hijack Marketing/Fake News:
Free of Risks—Never! 107
Hijack or Ambush Marketing 108
   All the Rage in 2010—The Soccer World Cup
   (in 2018, in Russia) and Ambush Marketing 109
How to Batten Down the Hatches 110

CHAPTER 11 .... **113**
Managing and "Exit" Control Long-Term 113
The Danger and the Consequences of the Exit Risks 116
Mitigation 117

CHAPTER 12 .... **119**
MiFID 2.0, Basel I, II and III etc. 119
Origins 119

Stress Testing the Banking System 120
    Black Swans and Nassim Nicolas Taleb 121
Basel IV—The Next Generation of RWA 122
    Finalising Basel III and Evolving Basel IV 122
Central Banking—The Future 123
Useful Further Reading 123
MifID—The Markets in Financial Instruments Directive 124
    Merger Risk 125

CHAPTER 13 127

InfoTech 127
Cyber Risks and Hackers 127
What is the "Cyber" Threat Exactly? 129
    Companies—Lipstick on their Collars 129
    Computers 130
    Cyber Marketing 130
Financial Payments System Links 130
International Balance of Payments Statistics 131
    Currency Weakness (and Strength) 131
Bond Issuance and Money Transfer-Related Fraud (Africa and the Americas) 132
Vanilla theft and Ransom 132
Financial Crime 132
Machine Growth—Intelligence Wise 134

Perilous 135
Approach 136

CHAPTER 14 137

Governance and Related Risks 137
The Crux—My Governance Issues 140
Private Companies' Governance 143
Public Sector Governance—Government? 144
Corporate Governance—A potted history 145
Corporate Governance 145
Historical Review 146
Walker Report 147
The Issue of Non-executives 149
The UK Corporate Governance Code of 2010 152
Conclusions 154

SUMMARY 157

APPENDIX 159

Brexit 159
Case studies 159
   Policies and People 159
   3G and 4G Sales of National Licenses to
   Telecoms Companies 160
   Risks in Bidding 161
   Facebook's Disastrous IPO 162

Elon Musk, 2018—A Turning Point for
the Serial Entrepreneur 164
Goldman Sachs, August 1998 165
Solyndra, June 2010 167
Prada, June 2011 168
Kozmo, March-August 2000 169
Harrah's/Caesar's Entertainment,
October–November 2010 169
STOP PRESS 170
More Lessons From (Elite) Sport 171
The Two Bs, Bury FC and Bolton Wanderers FC 171
Cricket . . . again 171
And—Rugby Union . . . again 172

BIBLIOGRAPHY 173

ACKNOWLEDGEMENTS

I WOULD LIKE TO sincerely thank several people for their help on this book, even if this help was indirect.

The first is my late father, who made me a small wooden platform on which I could place my laptop, surprisingly enough, to write the chapters so that I wouldn't hurt my back stooping to type. That was one risk dealt with!

The next is my ma, who always supports me even though right now she is suffering from the joint agony of severe shingles and a badly broken wrist, and of course, a broken heart after my father died. The thing I cherish about my mum is her stoic nature and her almost bloody-minded determination. She is a very strong lady, one who has stood by her man all her life and been a rock for my brother and me. She taught us all the domestic chores, ironing, cooking, cleaning and tidying (and of course filing and paperwork).

All the while my brother resided in Staines-Upon-Thames, looking after my father who was terminally ill with (prostate) cancer. My father, John Michael Peach, sadly passed away on 22nd June 2019. My mother and I miss his "larger than life presence" every day; he was a force to be reckoned with at home at work and in the car and latterly, even in bed!

The other helpers are all my mates from my City days:

Shaun Cutler, my long-suffering boss at NatWest Securities "brokers to the gentry".

William Forrester (Billy Bush), who amazingly said he'd be "honoured" to proofread the book.

Ian Hunt, my best mate from Sussex whose support since 1997 I couldn't have done without.

My eldest daughter Lexi for proofreading and arranging for her mum to do the same. She (Lee Masters) runs a hedge fund advisory service for Hedgemasters, her company, a partnership with her bestie mate Sarah Williamson.

Stephen McGoldrick, who's still an analyst at Deutsche Bank and may well be my co-author on editions 2 and 3, which will, thanks to Stephen, be a bit more technical and aimed at practitioners and academics. Sorry and please forgive me, Steve.

Adam Park, good lad.

Ian White, clever lad.

Cliff Fisher, I sincerely hope you read it, Cliff!

And finally, a (sort of) inspiration to me, Piers Lowson of Baillie Gifford, who put up with me as a telephone jockey in Edinburgh for a wee bit too long.

And finally- again, my youngest daughter Imogen, who is an anchor in my life and understands me as well as putting up with the mood swings when writers' block would strike!

Rob Peach

EXECUTIVE SUMMARY

RISK: To exactly where have we got to in the 21st century with (public) awareness of all types of risk? What they are, how to *"USE THEM"* [1], how to mitigate and control them, and finally how to find opportunity in them in a positive away rather than feel the threat. The purpose of the book is to set down a short, clear and concise guide to this landscape.

---

[1] This is the differentiating factor of this Handbook, seeing risk as opportunity as well as of course, threat.

KINDYNOS[2] OR KINDA LOSSES?—ALL ABOUT RISK 21C

Periculum

RISK MANAGEMENT HAS become a crucial activity for organisations and for macro-financial management over the past few decades, specifically since 1980. This handbook looks at the numerous types of risk that an organisation may be faced with, explores the universal analysis of risk in legible shorthand and examines risk management techniques to investigate how these organisations can systematically drive out, mitigate or eliminate risk, with the objective being to either drive out both financial and physical losses or the potential for them to occur. In the final chapter, we also look at how the protagonist can also use risk, treating it as an opportunity rather than a threat.

Now is the time to re-evaluate your approach to risk. Clarity of thought can help you and/or your organisation mitigate risk and preserve a competitive edge. If, like me, you have "auto-assumptions" brought about by habits and apathy, you might be in need of a May-time spring cleaning.

---

[2] Kindynos is the Greek word for "danger".

Clues to the characteristics of many risky behaviours are based in our anthropology and linguistics. Here's a true story[3]: Some 100 years ago, a consultant was hired to discover why there had been so many accidents, including some fatalities, at an oil plant. The assumptions about language were the key. Believe it or not, many smokers at the plant in question believed it unsafe to smoke akin a full barrel of oil, whilst all the same people believed that smoking was safe next to an *empty* barrel. The word "empty" to many meant safe; a hidden and flawed assumption, hence resulting in a high level of accident occurrence and many casualties. Oil residue equalled considerable residual, unrecognised risk.[4]

Danger is ubiquitous.

The Origins of Risk

"Risk management is the human attempt at bringing the future under control". *The Odyssey,* written by the inimitable Homer, has some lessons for us with respect to the above.

This handbook now takes the reader on a journey past many of the areas where a business (or a person) experiences risks, followed by some ideas on how to eliminate or mitigate them.

---

[3] *Risk: Why Smart People Have Dumb Accidents*—Steve Casner—Mentioned by Gillian Tett *FTWeekend* article dated 23rd June 2018.

[4] Gillian Tett, *Financial Times* November 2018.

CHAPTER 1

Context of Risk

Facilis descensus averno, (translated: Easy was the descent to Hell)

Virgil, circa 19 to 29BC[5]

Consideration

Risk is always opportunity as well as threat; the secret being to dissect, divide and conquer. This fact is often overlooked as people who observe from the outside looking in are often glass-half-empty types. The landscape of risk can have a sky-blue horizon, beckoning us if we treat her with respect.

E.M. Forster and Others

"How do I know what I think until I see (or write) what I say"? This, in the context of this risk analysis teaches us that

---

[5] Virgil: The Aeneid

things will always appear clearer with the aid of some deeper analysis. E.M. Forster was a deep 'un. His *Passage to India* was a profound novel exploring the human psyche through a touristy ramble through the Indian countryside. People miss things when they do not look beyond skin-deep. Therefore, underneath there may well be upside and opportunity as well as the (more obvious) hazards and risks.

R.C. Collingwood was an Englishman and an FBA (Fellow of the British Academy). I think we should endeavour to set this person's background also:

- He lived from 1889 until 1943; that's until he was just 54 years old.
- He *is* remembered as a philosopher, a historian, and an archaeologist.
- Could one find this person a more educated friend? I doubt it.

To follow this properly, please read Lawrence Stone's *Tristram Shandy*.

Collingwood had a special mind with regard to risk management, advocating "thinking the past within the context of one's own experience" and implying the need for a *constant* replaying of events to crystallise their context and evidence vigilance and care, the essentials of sound management of risk.

The Czech Republic

The switch from believers and some would say moot images is arguably almost complete in the former Czechoslovakia. In and around 1989 as the Berlin Wall came down, there was much agitation afoot in Europe. Thus, in January 1993, there was a "peaceful dissolution[6]" of Czechoslovakia into the Czech Republic and Slovakia.

In the face of change (and to an extent, a revolution), things have to suddenly morph into new existences. Again, the relevance to risk here is that this can and does happen overnight. The adaptation process has to be instantaneous and can be painful. In trying to mitigate this type of risk, it is not always possible to put in place contingency plans when time is short and change is momentous. One just has to reactively cope—a modern phenomenon that is coming closer to being a norm. Seat-of-the-pants management style, some might say.

Another quote to consider:

> *"The Leaning Wall falls at the touch a finger,"* meaning a little effort can pay very significant dividends. The major lesson here for our analysis is the constant need for patience, or in many a case, attempting to completely nullify impatience. With a stepped/chunked down approach, one comes to realise that the smallest change will precipitate the transformation. Learning and coping with this comes with experience.

The right word at the right time not only sets us free but the improvement is (always) sustainable.

"Getting and spending we lay waste our Powers" said by Wordsworth and quoted From Mike Brearley The cricketer's *On Form*. Wordsworth implies that the risk of being materially minded manifests itself in a thwarting or individual potency and competence. This as per the rather incisive former cricket captain is typically profound. Brearley is a practicing

---

[6] https://en.wikipedia.org/wiki/Dissolution_of_Czechoslovakia

psychotherapist and has had a long and challenging career long since he left Lord's cricket ground as a player for the last time. Interestingly, with his insight and skill Brearley never went into the coaching arena; by the looks of things he was and is too busy with more pressing matters.

Poem

> "He who binds to himself a joy does the winged life destroy,
> But he who kisses the joy as it flies,
> Lives in ETERNITY'S sunrise."
>
> —Blake W.

The relevance here, and mantra indeed, is to always stay curious, keep active and change as the times demand. In this lies "joy", for which I read as self-actualisation. Quitting is always a particularly weak option but one that I think has validity in certain situations. Seth Godin majors on this in his short publication *The Dip*. There is an old saying that "quitters never win and winners never quit;" this is incorrect, Godin claims, since even the best winners quit all the time. This is called "prioritisation". It is the case from the smallest endeavour like brushing one's teeth right up to the big stuff, such as building a large shopping centre or motorway.

Where stress, for example, is savaging your day on a regular basis, throw the towel in and get away from the frustrations. You will then see from a distance after the relevant time-period that you did the correct thing. Try not to make a habit of this, however; since it does not assist in longevity, which employers still like (in spite of their own disloyalty). That is, of course, if you still respect employers well enough to serve them!

The Hardest Thing of All

Abraham Lincoln as I saw him. Cl R Peach 29 January 2018.

Lincoln as a leader showed us more about risk than any other post-revolution leader in history. He managed the country through the American Civil War and during the most severe moral, constitutional and political crisis, as we can say now with the benefit of hindsight in peace time. He strategically guided tens of thousands of troops at any one time. He was in charge of the Union's singular military strategy and clearly had a nose for perilous situations. It was in his job title to "confiscate and free slaves who were used to support the Confederate war effort." In practice, the law had little effect, but it did signal political support for abolishing slavery in the

Confederacy. This would have been controversial at the time and Lincoln has to be congratulated for navigating himself and most of the Union through these crises and risks; physical and otherwise.

Abraham Lincoln was assassinated by well-known stage actor John Wilkes Booth in 1865. The assassin was part of a larger collaboration whose aim was the revival of the Confederacy. In the words borrowed from the knowledge website Wikipedia's entry, "Beyond Lincoln's death, the plot failed," this being indicative of Lincoln's overall influence.

Reputational Risk

Intangible assets constitute some 80% of many a company's book value. Two things create growth in a company's intangible assets. First, many companies begin brand-building and effective PR that grows their market capitalisation on the world's stock exchanges. Secondly, speculation by investors can fuel stock prices; when given a value, the premium over net assets is termed "intangible assets".

On 6 February, 2018, and during the preceding 48 hours, stock markets around the world reeled. This pattern repeated every few months, including September and into October 2018, with brokers putting out stark warnings about how much of America's population had begun trading in its pension and future security for CASH now and (of course) to take care of their children who can't get a job or on the property ladder.

Collapse is a threat as the world realises that the Donald Trump era perhaps brings more doubt than prosperity over the longer-term horizon; especially when one considers the US/Chinese trade wars that were initiated by the former reality TV show host. Trump cut his teeth in a business that he inherited; this factor alone invalidates his authenticity, as his behaviour thus far demonstrates. The man lacks integrity and discretion as his Twitter account murmurings show us. So, with markets in medium term jittery mode thus far as I write, we ask, "How far south will the establishment allow markets to take us?"

Reputation is all. Remind me of all the times you have ticked *"word of mouth"* after being asked "How did you hear about us"? This occurrence adheres itself to the same Pareto principle, the 80:20 rule.[7]

Word of Mouth Now and Henceforth—Digging Deeper

By 2027, it is arguable that being allocated a "Like" by a Facebook or LinkedIn connection may be more important than receiving a magazine or newspaper endorsement is in 2018. The pairs of eyes, more restless and numerous, might just lead to the break that makes the difference between our comprehension and perception of value now, as opposed to what it may become in the future. 2027 is not so distant.

The questions that are on my mind more perhaps than any other current dilemma is: Twenty years from now, is our monitoring and evaluation tool going to be social media? Shall its significance dwarf other distribution outlets? Traditional media may well have been sabotaged fatally by this time and public opinion thus will be "all over the place". Nomadic but... with or without the common sense?

Twitter and Facebook or multiple "shares" on LinkedIn is

---

[7] The Pareto principal was noticed and established in the late nineteenth century by Vilfredo Pareto and is ably reviewed by Robert Sanders of the Rogers Corporation in US in his book entitled *The Pareto Principle: Its Use and Abuse*.

what I am talking about. As Julia Hobsbawm discussed and imparted her experience of **"networking"**, interpersonal and technological, building a social infrastructure that will reliably support you after a stumble or push you forward onto the front foot as you are gaining confidence is critical. Thorough networking is the "hard skin" that we all need as a firm base to take and to give criticism with meaning to back it up. The social media world is very noisy; networking can be quietly confident as well as enjoyable. It is, in and of itself a defence against reputational risk, social and professional detachment.

The secondary and tertiary connections made by your connections—hundreds, maybe thousands of people that you have never met—will be the key to opening opportunity and future wealth. In order to "get supported", the crucial factor is telling people about what, who and how you know. In a world chock-full with infotech and information, your ability to read, filter and digest and send it on is the factor that is currently known as "X". A stable network is one critical risk mitigator for all, I plead: get building!

In a recent publication, *Deep Thinking* by the former chess GM (grand master), Garry Kasparov compares the reproductive gene for information to Moore's Law, or, the ability to store, transfer and reproduce vast amounts of data by one push of the index finger. *"Most of all, computers get stronger,"* he says, and what he doesn't mention is that this means they go faster and sweep information about your personae from all over the planet; this is now irrefutable truth.

"Doctor You", proclaims *The Economist* in March 2018, as technology makes self-healthcare ever easier. Babylon Healthcare is another example of how technology can and will revolutionise the health and pharmaceuticals sectors. Babylon brings healthcare experts online using basic messaging technology, the complexity necessary when addressing healthcare issues comes from the knowledge of the medics. Through taking a doctor-patient meeting out of the equation, it strips out a layer of expense that typifies the managerial UK's NHS, which from a "customer's[8]" perspective gives the impression that the right hand does not know what the left hand is doing. It certainly remains to be seen whether Dr Ali Parsa[9] will convert the tech-led model to be successful. In a healthcare concern such as this one, success should *not* be measured in profitability terms.

To digress a little, the author and much-renowned academic Daniel C. Dennett has recently written *Bacteria to Bach and Back* which is extensive coverage of "consciousness" in the human race and far beyond. In the context of the power of Gordon Moore's Law[10], it adds to my fear (and hope indeed!) that we are dealing with an irresistible force that is technology and science. It will solve the dilemmas that come with aging in the longer term, but that is a discussion for another day. Dennett's work has been published in many languages and I would urge that you have a look.

The Phenomenon that is the Game of Cricket

Through anecdotal hearsay and the genuine ability to witness cricket, one conclusion is that taking a batsman's wicket is a blessing, and a rare one, too. The batsman's eternal task is to evaluate risk and avoid physical injury. It is a demanding occupation, added to which in Twenty20 (a much shorter

---

[8]   For customer read "patient".

[9]   Dr Ali Parsa- Chief Executive Officer, Babylon Healthcare Inc.

[10] Moore's Law: the number of transistors in a dense integrated circuit doubles about every two years.-Power indeed.

version of cricket) (s)he is expected to score at high speed and run like a hurricane between the wickets; like baseball, but running 22 yards in a straight line repetitively, rather than running a longer distance in a circle.

In all climates, including those in the imminent future, the cricketers are not permitted to endure torrential rain. Thinking about the injurious hazard, I am drawn to ask, "Why should this **ever** hold up play?" We have built tunnels across and underneath the globe and a few drops of rain can stop us playing with a bat and ball in a field? Really? Surely the human race can overcome this minor inconvenience to the favour of enhanced enjoyment for the long-suffering fans that travel miles to these games and pay on average around £100+ per ticket for a match in England.

Cricket's beauty, trickery and complexity can be viewed through this lens:

"To trick a clear-sighted batter[11] *it is easy, to sustain the trickery, to confuse and confound the batsmen and to even turn down the lights whilst doing so . . . now that is skill with that small round number!"*

To round off these cricketing analogies, it is necessary to bring a few risk-related thoughts into focus. The batsmen's raison detre is to keep batting and scoring for as long as possible in all forms of the game. This requires patience, stamina and a calm disposition and temperament. Seeing the ball bowled slower than expected and floating towards the batsman, the

---

[11] Ms Anya Shrubsole and her World Cup winning ladies' team, have cemented cricket as truly all-inclusive, she then appeared on the front cover of the coveted Wisden Almanack 2018—Done!

latter must keep a cool head and play each ball on its merits, avoiding fielder traps and making it to the end of the over (six, usually over-arm bowls).

Compare this to the quarterly rush for earnings numbers and the tendency to "window dress" at Christmas[12]. The analogy comes into its own here. In order to accumulate runs, the batsman's choice of shot is all-important. In order to accumulate FUM (funds under management), individual stock selection is what matters. In both scenarios, analysis and narrowing down thought processes is important. It can also be stressed at this stage that both are young people's games; sport has a lifespan of fifteen years in terms of an expected player's career. Fund management—and, for example, brokering and selling—and indeed trading are around the same mark of fifteen years max. Survivors beyond this time horizon are prodigiously talented and are usually rewarded as such.

Back in the world of the banks, during 2006 and 2007 in the run-up to new BIS[13] Basel III (3.0) legislation (which is that affecting the Bank of International Settlements), the financial institutions of the globe were furiously lobbying the European Commission and Union to more readily share our data with commercial, consumer and retail outlets to free up

---

[12] The year-end for the fund manager is his raison detre. He is paid in the case of hedge funds on percentage performance and in the case of a vanilla fund manager, he is remunerated on the increase in "funds under management" so year end mark to market and new monies around this time are what he gets paid on, bonus to boot.

[13] The BIS—Bank of International Settlements which "settles all transactions between the entire globe's market participants" (counterparties as they are known).

data exchange between transactors in order to oil the wheels of global capitalism in a world that believed boom-bust was a thing of the past[14]. Then the sub-prime crises and relentless credit crunches all over the globe started to happen. In a reactive and corruption-free world, a severity which was fatal could have been avoided; alas not.

So in early 2018, in the exhausting, yet indefatigable climb up to the next fall (credit crunch 2.0), here we are letting banks freely share our data and trying to explain to their (many) often octogenarian customers what an API is—seriously! An Application Program Interface is crucial to gaining access to technological gateways through the awkwardness of secured coding. Confused? You will be! If you remember your first cash card, the four-figure code required is what we are focusing on here. Human behaviour being what it is, with Alan Turing in mind, we all have to set out to learn all we can. The current advent of artificial intelligence and its many implications for data and personal security are one of the key areas to focus on if you're in your thirties and working in the risk, operations or HR functions. AI will doubtless have some effects that we have not thought of yet.

The process of transmuting vast amounts of the over-fifties onto the internet and onto emails and smart phones is an uphill struggle not just for banks but for all businesses, but we will just have to accept that it's going to get easier and that it will take a

---

[14] This was a somewhat politically rhetorical and false proclamation by the 2008-10 Prime Minister Gordon Brown who was the long-standing previous Chancellor of the Exchequer under Mr Blair's "New Labour" administration. It was their laissez-faire approach to Banking legislation that ushered through the calamity.

long time. A parallel fact is that in a cashless society up to **eight million** Britons would struggle to survive[15].

To their credit (boom-boom), many people over sixty do not use the APIs in question nor do they surf the internet; but now, of course, nearly everyone else does. Hence my supressed fear of contagion when the next crunch begins. This prediction is as certain as night following day because the banks (including the Central Banks) are much more in the driver's seat now than they were back in 2007; moral compasses have gone seriously awry to allow this to happen. Danger is lurking beneath outwardly calm transactional markets.

In 2008, I remember predicting a trifle naïvely that credit crunch number two would occur in 2012. I was, it seems, at least five years out, because with the hikes in interest rates by the Federal Reserve in the United States and the (mini) crisis at—among many others—Provident Financial, the makings of the next crisis are **firmly** in the pipeline. The Brexit impact for the UK is yet to be determined and the negotiating stance of the UK seems to get ever softer and more expensive by the day. If there was a "no deal" scenario, this may ignite a volatile market correction. Uncertainty could reign and markets despise uncertainty. The change in Prime Minister in July 2019 marks a crucial turning point in the European negotiating situation. As the *Spectator* points out (week 2, August 2019), the European project is a political one above all else and the way Greece in 2014 had a second referendum and despite its "Grexit" verdict, Yanis Varoufakis blinked and the Euro-political project rumbled on, Greece remained and remains in the Euro—currency and Union.

The background of quasi US/China tariff wars may not

---

[15] *Financial Times* Money 3 March 2019.

help the "political risk situation" especially as it is still present towards the fall of 2019. The change that has come with the arrival of Mr Boris Johnson in UK as Prime Minister currently appears as if long transition periods will not be fudged into the solution to the Brexit dilemma. Markets and politicians continue to display nervousness; the pound is still vulnerable even though it has already dropped significantly in value against Euro and US Dollar alike. This though is helping exports and inward investments. Despite what entrenched *Financial Times* authors say, as well as staunch remainers like Phillip Hammond, it is not *all bad*. The payment of the £1bn bribe to the Ulster Unionists was blatant, but as Johnson strives to remove "the backstop", his majority in the house moves down to ONE. Politicians around the two major political parties have now created significant risk, such that a Government of Unity is being broached, a landmark move indeed, away from the United Kingdom's two-party "system".

Both the UK's and the US' retail sectors are in big trouble; in the UK, British Home Stores went bankrupt, Pound World into administration, the John Lewis chain's sales are flat-lining and Tesco are extremely busy buying up residential land and trying to dovetail in shops behind them. Corporate greed and desperation have set into retailers' roots. This and other reversals of fortune are being covered up studiously by the elites. I sent my predictive note to Gillian Tett, who wrote *Fools' Gold,* the story of the 2007-08 crash and the reason for it. She remains the US editor of the newspaper and was sanguine about my opinion—why not send her to the new nexus of influence, China? Maybe, but with North Korea ongoing she may not want to be there with her children.

She disagreed with my forecast but did express a passing

acknowledgement of my sagacity—she thought the cracks would start appearing further into the future, and so it has transpired.

She was cautious but not as panicky as me; I guess this comes with journalistic experience.

CHAPTER 2

Back to Reputation

THE RELENTLESS DRIVE of information technology will never leave off. History teaches us this. Trying to stop it would be like protesting against electric current back in the day—somewhat misguided in a historical context. Pushing water uphill without a pipe.

As *The Economist* recently pointed out[16] (though not as forcefully as necessary), the virtual business model hides a catalogue of ills from chronic employment insecurity right through the multitude of maleficent knock-on effects including deficient customer service. Nationalisation, renationalisation in fact grew more likely by the day as Carillion, Centrica (formerly British Gas) and the major water franchises look more likely to fail as profit-making entities. There is always this conflict between private ownership[17]—and its requisite profitability—and the provision of a public good. The factor that is tested to

---

[16] *Economist Journal*: January 18, 2018.

[17] Richard Rorty: "Private obsession fulfils public need" 1989.

the extreme and the measure of political persuasion one way or the other is the struggle of the worker—labour as a factor of production.

One company that seems to consistently skirt around the regulators' scrutiny is British Telecom—BT. Its incursion into the sports TV market is decimating the in-person cricket and rugby audience and upsetting clubs like Manchester United and Chelsea FC. The risks are manifold; the company's position is way too powerful and its shameless constant lobbying of the government officials that look after it is not to be ignored. Its reputation depends on which consumers are consulted... many find the company's sharp practices repulsive and, interestingly, its CEO[18] has stepped aside. The board seem aware of problems into the future. It should, I believe, be broken up. It is a monopoly that shouldn't be allowed to continue.

Beyond the power and reach of Moore's Law lies the next big thing that probably only a handful of Silicon Valley scientists know about. I refer here to AI—the "threat" of artificial intelligence. Either way, upon its landscape shall lie many a tattered reputation. As I reminded in the introduction, this also represents an opportunity.

In all walks of life, however, there are saboteurs; people like hijack marketers and modern-day populist "photo-bombers" who get an inexplicable thrill out of spoiling everything for other people. Many a saboteur will stop at nothing.

What to do? Well, start by investing in anti-virus software to prevent the aforementioned hacking. Then I think that it is a case of monitoring and often scanning your social media streams. If you come across abuse and covert sabotage, use

---

[18] Gavin Patterson to step down as BT CEO, June 08 2018.

the platform's reporting mechanisms to let the watchdog or the police know. Do not be backward in coming forward; remember, it is your (company's) reputation on the line.

If you are selling product online and you notice the hashtag #badservice, it means that somebody is not happy with your product or attendant services. Try to nip this in the bud, quickly, by over delivery on the very next interaction with them. If you do this well, you may be rewarded by some positive leverage of "word of mouth" referral, a virtuous circle of praise rippling through other people's networks. Marvellous.

As the human hands over more control faculties to algorithms and machines—I'm typing this on a phone and predictive text is helping me on almost every word!—we must realise that this is a chance to "rise above" and plan to do more, effectively and less wastefully.

Technology, Trust and Reputation

Banks have enough to concern them without adding an imminent threat to their system security. Currently, NatWest Bank's reputation is at a low point and its recent advertising strapline "We are what we do" is inappropriate since too many expletives spring readily to mind when hearing it. I will elaborate.

There has been a share price rally recently (June 2018) but this will last only until the government lightens up on its 83% and onerous stake in this still "publicly owned" company. It mystifies me that we, the people, own the majority of the equity, yet there is *not a trace of public ownership at board level*. This loads a large risk right onto the government's shoulders. It is the public, however, who will take the hit on the losses. These are not paper losses; they are hefty cash losses that will swell the UK's deficit. The same traditional self-interested drivers are in play whilst this ludicrous situation is allowed to continue. In 2019, the company supposedly turned a corner with profitability returning. It is not beyond the realm of possibility that as soon as "black" returns to the balance sheet, the government will press the "sell" button on its stake. Employees and pension holders (in whose ranks I number) should watch this space; the privatised entity may not have the stomach to take back the significant pension liabilities.

Barclays Bank is another finance company whose reputation has been somewhat sullied, first by substantial rumour that it distributed bribes into the Middle East to secure bail-out funding as an alternative to governmental cash, which many others settled for back in 2008-09[19]. Second, by the shamefaced behaviour of its former chief executive, Bob Diamond. Diamond is far from ashamed, given that he now runs an agency and consultancy stalking around all his old contacts and contracts! Ex-chief executive John Varley has also been implicated in the scurrilous behaviour.

Two banks are breaking the mould and becoming successful for doing so, shoving along the status quo, changing the customer experience—looking at the basics. Both newcomers have adopted a more paper and people-oriented business. These are Richard Branson's Virgin Money and a relatively recent arrival, the innovative Metro Bank. They are direct beneficiaries from the fallout in trust and respect that we used to have for the big four financiers: Barclays, RBS/NatWest, HSBC and Lloyds. A fifth financier should also be remembered, the Spanish outfit Banco Santander. More recent press murmurings suggest

---

[19] Patrick Jenkins, *Financial Times*. "Conduct in Business Needs Regulating like Conduct in Banking" 15 April 2019. The "bribe" is alleged to have been £322 million.

that Metro Bank has run into difficulty. Some six months ago, their liquidity position had come into question in speculative coverage, but since then on into 2019, market fears have been allayed.

Connectivity and the Threat that it Poses

It cannot be denied that ten years after the crises of systemic confidence, thanks to quantitative easing we have to date averted it, and to put it in layman's terms, we've put off the day of reckoning by a decade or so[20]. The crucial question is how long can asset managers put off investors' ill will created by lower bond returns and yields as well as sideways equity markets? Experts proclaimed during the first quarter of 2018 that volatility will be a feature of equity markets from now on; we have had a prolonged absence, after all. Each lull in volatility quells journalistic pens; these writers are anxious and, in my opinion, rightly so.

With enhanced influence and control over their central banks, the retail bank sector seems intent on bringing everything online. This despite a distinct uptick in fraud levels created by hackers and internet tricksters. My personal email is bombarded daily with fake Amazon invoices for me to dispute, the idea being that one puts one's debit card details into the laptop only to find money minus rather than money plus.

Coupled with this, contactless cards are stolen in vast quantities every day, the £30 single transaction not really

---

[20] The Federal Reserve began raising rates in order to quell inflationary pressures. However, under considerable pressure from President Trump, this cautionary activity has been halted. WTS—watch this space—the next move and the one thereafter will be indicative of (despairing) government policy.

stemming people's ambitions; fraudulent aspirations. ApplePay has a higher transactional limit and seems safe—for now. It relies on fingerprint, the nearest to DNA we can get for the smartphone. Many still use a PIN code instead, which has more risk of duplication and fraud attached.

Concurrently, people in influential places (the havens of capital) have begun investing in virtual or "crypto-currencies", though I feel by early 2019 the speculative frenzy is past its peak. Bitcoin has exchanged for anything between $400 and $4400 recently, the hype around its "universal adoption" obviously driving some highly dangerous behaviours among speculators and (probably) many a hedge fund—are all driven by momentum trading.

Employee Exploitation Über Alles

Mr Travis Kalanick, the now-former CEO of Über and serial entrepreneur, stood aside from the company in 2017 after a sustained period of lobbying/harrying by acknowledged governance aces and journalists, all of whom had spotted the flaws in the ways and the culture of management that were marring corporate productivity. Every "ism" you could think of was throwing the company into disarray: demonstrable sexism and abuse of young "employees", ageism right down to the early recruitment process and racism, with blatant sexism reputedly to the fore.

Now all of this is interesting when placed in contrast with corporate cultures of the same ilk; one example springing to mind is Airbnb, whose culture is young (in corporate age), yet conversant with the media and collaborative in a collegiate style.

The technology company status of these has moved, arguably established them, from a real estate company to a technology giant in Airbnb's case and from a transportation company's identity in Uber's case. This is what Linda Gratton called *"The Shift"*: *the future of work demands flexibility-maximum for payment and loyalty-minimum*, in a world transformed by technological dominance.

It is my belief that the technology behind electricity generation and battery life shall be crucial for the success of the next generation of many advances. This "makings of a story" is reinforced in a recent *Electrical Worker* article which emphasizes the importance of addressing this. [21] The grid in the UK is dwarfed by that in the mighty US, the issue, risks and some of my concerns are addressed at the link in the footnote below.

You've Done Too Much, Much Too Young . . .

Thanks to these fast and early transitions in technology from one so-called revolution to the next, we will fret more over our children's safety and wellbeing—in that order. The Internet has ushered in an era where even the slightest interaction online could spell danger for a person under the age of 18. Statistics show us that sex, abuse and drug-related crime are not any more present in 2019 than they were, for example, in the mid- to late-nineteen sixties, the baby-boomer epoch. We do have more eventualities to fret upon. Grooming, cyber-crime, cyber-bullying and false impersonations trick our offspring into exposing all their own

---

[21] International Brotherhood of Electrical Workers, "Fixing the Grid's #1 Problem". *The Electrical Worker Online*, July 2019. http://www.ibew.org/articles/19ElectricalWorker/EW1907/index.html

frailties and weaknesses, part them from significant funds, and elicit data from them under false pretences; all are clear and present dangers in which safeguarding and parenting must be front of mind.

The young human race must re-learn what it is that remains *their private property*. Facebook, Twitter and even LinkedIn persuade people to provide swathes of private data and to share it with the world. For this to happen in 2019 is high risk. ***Even your very identity is as risk***. Now, a recent *Economist* study revealed, by just recording a few seconds (7) of someone's vocal footage, one can steal one's way in to or through another's financial firewall. Voice recognition technologies can be thus compromised and identities stolen. This is worrisome.

It's not what the young have "done" intentionally, it is what they are doing accidentally. Even an innocent thing like placing your email or mobile address on a social media site can invite the undesirable visitors to your (parents') front door. This too is scary.

As a risk management professional, I admit that my bias is more caution versus less, but I do come from a sensible place on this and I have read enough case studies to make my skin crawl. As parents, we all have a duty to safeguard our children's data online, when underneath the angst we suspect that the internet should be policed much better. We are where we are: it isn't.

Corporate Social Responsibility 2019 and Beyond

Paper on CSR as Risk Management 2005

There have been a few salient papers with such subject matter but this one stands out:

> *Corporate Social Responsibility as Risk Management—* (2005), Kytle B and Ruggie JG: Harvard

"Going global" necessitates bearing social risk and doing so competently. The subtitle for this paper is "A Model for Multinationals", so there is a clear target subject and audience here.

Since the advent of the "multinational proper" this risk—attaching to the social—has been ignored by the companies' sector; they have—simplistically speaking—been too busy making money and hiking prices to consider social impact. Plastics, CO_2 and non-biodegradables spring to consciousness.

It is a disputed point. Some thirty to forty years after CSR was first mentioned, it should have become embedded into corporate culture—it simply hasn't. It is still subject to "environmental and employee benefits washing", i.e. pretending to do CSR and reporting it but spending little capital upon the projects. Companies partake in greenwashing; environmental window-dressing. They also hold token development programmes for employees such as fundraising days and provide external volunteering opportunities. However, in the course of day-to-day working, all employees are expected to contribute several "pounds of flesh" and loyalty by the employer in its turn cannot be expected. Loyalty reciprocity lies in the gutter; it is a private sector one-way street.

Decision making at company level now has myriad (social) risks attached. Given that many companies often by chance end up trading internationally, the crossing of continents brings risks that were scarcer until the 1980s. By doing what it has done internationally, the corporate entity attracts more stakeholders that have been, to date, "aliens" of its business model. This, added to social media's impact, exponentially magnifies business and social risks.

The "CSR as Risk" paper positions corporate social responsibility AS risk management, implying that it can mitigate over ninety percent of all business risks with effective

CSR programmes. This in turn implies that most business risks are socially related and that, with the coming dominance of social media and to an extent, artificial intelligence (AI), this does indeed tend toward a truism. A fact one might argue.

"CSR-embedded practices provide the framework and principles for stakeholder engagement." Thus this paper again rings truer now than it did back in the 2000s when it was published.

If executed properly, they are a thermometer for the social temperature that will affect the business model. Though the governments of the world have lowered geographical and trade barriers between many countries, it is also true that the major driver of "globalization" per se is the private sector, which itself drives inequality and the exploitation of the neediest in societies.

Policing the Internet—Widening the Net?

Google, Amazon, Apple and Facebook have risen to be the paragons of inequality, monopolising the cash floating around right across the consumer economy, and quite simply, even with some hefty acquisitions, hoarding the proceeds on their balance sheets which have never hoarded so much of the folding stuff. Nor have these individuals and companies been fairly taxed on the income, if taxed at all. Amazon Europe is registered in Luxembourg and with its revenues its chief risk (technology aside) is tax-take. On 2017-18 revenues of £21.6bn, it paid a mere £16.5m. That is less than 0.076%. The company has steadfastly avoided that risk, much to the chagrin of authorities the world over. See how risks skew away from the wealthy as they employ their reserves in studied evasion.

The Internet needs regulation and in Margrethe Vestager

the EU has somebody who thinks the answer is simply to slap enormous fines on the techno-sector giants. The Americans—while engaging in hegemonic activities and lording it over hapless quasi-criminals—think individual governments need to focus on the abusers' activities in and beyond its own boundaries. That affects their citizens and denizens and they must start imposing boundaries and fines to temper the American dominators. Vestager has, in this context, at least made a start.

Issues of the Day: Cryptocurrencies—Hype or Fair Value?

After some arduous days closely watching others at my desk trading over the counter (OTC) and exchange traded futures, I remember that fair value[22] always hovered around the mark; that is, they were not speculated up exponentially as the bitcoins—usefully described as virtual, internet currencies of this world—have been. Ethereum and others have "bubble and bust" tendencies, prompting the Chinese government to authoritatively step in and ban ICOs (International Coin Offerings), the sale of the web "coins"—in oxygen form rather than paper or physical shares—to the public. It is the world's best attempt to move away from paper and coinage towards paperless electronic transfer. The move away from the gold standard is still being sustained to little effect; we are hooked on cash and high-viz bank balance checks. There seems little alternative despite recent inventions.

---

[22] The accurate value of the index in X months' time given the current rates of interest and the current dividend yield of the FTSE100 Index.

A consensus is bound to evolve around one of these "virtual currencies" but not any time soon. The speculators continue in thrall (to themselves of course). The governments of the world, in silent collusion with central banks, are to go about "chipping" cash, according to some eminently believable conspiracists. So cashless society is destination 2050 perhaps. Doubts still linger.

As markets took a ten-percent-plus correction in early 2018, crypto activities accompanied frenzied market trading. Germany, Italy and the UK, to name just three, are hobbling along in hung parliaments; 2018 should go down in history as the year of the politico's come-uppance, but then I would say that the politicians have had their day in the sun.

How to Stop Amazon From Continuing to Sell Everything and Buying All Its Competition

At 33 years old, some twentysomething years ago, I had an eureka moment at work (some three days into a new company employer's engagement with me), then I crawled into a hole in a specialist psychiatric hospital. My eureka was "telecoms club" as I envisioned a soon-to-be realised connected world that would disintermediate us humans. Needless to say that the prior sentence is written with some twenty-and-a-half years' benefit of hindsight. My feeble mind had leapt ahead a decade and my psychological status quo could not cope with it. I broke down for three months.

Now, of course, if anyone over eleven years old wants to talk to anyone, they Facebook, buy anything they please on Amazon, or purchase any specialist technology through Apple or Samsung. So five to ten private companies domiciled in America dominate over half of the world, by value anyway, since there are more people but less investment capital available in the countries of Asia that concern us: China and India, probably, but not in that order.

The workspaces of individuals and entire families, including all the student communities among us, have changed. This is one of the multitude of reasons for the "growth" of the cell phone, i.e. they all have bigger screens because people are living much of their lives on them.

As Ryanair in 2018 cancelled tens of thousands of flights[23] and EasyJet seems to go from strength to strength (www.easyeverything.com) one of the company's competitors, Monarch Air, ceased trading 2 Oct, 2017. Barely an eyebrow was raised; it ran, at the time in question, a 1990s business model in a 2030s world.

The Überization[24] of the economy dictates that Amazon's power shall continue growing, but rather worryingly there seems to be no credible alternative. I would advocate going to individual brands and sellers and patiently registering as a purchaser and not parting with our debit cards' details until we have kicked the tyres at least once. Maybe this last factor is dictating our propensity *not* to diversify our buying habits, or indeed to extend the £30 contactless (debit) card limit; a move in this direction is patently expected but the weaker communities have my support and many other millions like me, I hope. A significant increase in the limit would open the fraud floodgates for sure.

Whilst in a wealthy township in Berkshire at the weekend, some partygoers were outside fumbling with their mobile

---

[23] It is (the consensus) that the final number was 753,000 flights globally in a short time.

[24] '"Uber lifts lid on its losses as it plans listing" *Daily Telegraph* Business section 12th April 2019.

telephones. "Uber?" I enquired. I thought their licence has been revoked (court decision dated 22 September, 2017, not in Reading).

"They've brought the drivers in to do the job" one replied. QED, Uber over all! In late June 2018, Uber regained its London licence, despite vehement protests from many a more traditional quarter. Capitalism won out; the tech firm overcame its doubters—with ease. Lawyers' palms would have been well greased to mitigate Uber's exposures, a sure thing. Whilst weighing inequality against justice, one has always to bear in mind that capitalism will always win out against the (wo)man on the street.

Sporting Examples

When considering sport, any sport, the prime drivers (for risk and commitment) are motivation and passion. Now, as most protagonists are younger than previously, this is itself driving the fact that winners are ever younger. Roger Federer at 37 years young has pocketed twenty Grand Slam titles, whilst—at the other end of the fortune tightrope—Michael Schumacher, still a young man, remains just about alive after a skiing accident. He is just 50 years old.

MIKE BREARLEY
ON FORM

J.M. Brearley, *On Form* cover, Little Brown 2017
"This man has a degree in people" Mr Rodney Hogg
(Australian pace bowler, 1979.)

Politicians

The laying of power at the feet of a Jeremy Corbyn would be fatal for the Kingdom with the line-up of ineptitude behind him. None have had sensible grafting jobs or, needless to say, apprenticeships; some are surprisingly youthful. These errant power brokers all have a role to play, however, as Labour will soon come to the fore. It is the understated precursor to many a news bulletin and documentary.

The risk to the UK here is having an incoming administration on a thin majority which has clear ideas about policy: costly renationalisation of many utilities, dilating budget deficits and no experience of implementing policies through an entrenched civil service which would make it more than a little awkward for them. McDonnel and Corbyn would struggle, one should not doubt.

Reputations of the elites in Britain that are the politicians lie in tatters. The Brexit vote has brought out the worst; right across the political divide, parties individually are divided. The Labour party is split in two; on the left, the Corbynista Communists and to the right, the more fascist-inclined "social democrats". On the right still further, we have the hard Brexit Tories, now led from the front by Mr Boris Johnson. Negotiations in 2019 become ever stickier and a "fudge" to avoid market disruptions and volatile market downward corrections seems inevitable.

Conservatives—The Reputation Dilemma

Former leader, Theresa May, a vicar's daughter with zero business experience and few social skills or graces, addressed the October 2017 party conference—weakly. Her voice died almost on cue for all those who prayed for her failure. In terms of substance, this speech was sparse. One of the pledges was to address "vested interests", yet she absolutely lauded the free market and the private sector's effectiveness and "earning prowess"; my words, not hers.

It is and ever was the private sector's ability to generate wealth that accrues a tax reserve that pays directly and indirectly for all the public services (and servants).

The Tories' reputation itself is that of volatility. This is due to the inherent disloyalty and infighting over Europe and policy in general. One half of the party remains steadfastly anti-

Europe whilst the other half, led by erstwhile Chancellor of the Exchequer Kenneth Clarke, wants to embrace the bureaucracy and remain in the European Union and the single market and have no limits on the movement of people. David Cameron, now long gone from British politics, called the referendum in a moment of madness which he thought mistakenly that the resounding success of "remain" would solve the party's historic ills forever. His abrupt departure was a precursor to a period of prolonged uncertainty and political weakness of resolve. In 2019, this uncertainty continues unabated, a risk to all of us in the UK.

Switching attention to what is crucial economically at this juncture, in the words of one wealthy asset manager who used to run a financial brokerage in the City, where I once worked—he interviewed me more than once for the role and I was successful: "The Chinese are buying up everything at the moment." We were actually talking about a venture that I was very nearly recruited for, a breakneck speed attempt on the world land-speed record by a reputable company that straddles charity, automobiles and education. The Chinese largesse in Africa and on the Asian subcontinent is the chief risk to the West and the best that America has yet come up with is a weak alliance with North Korea, followed by the makings of a trade war with China. Imaginative stuff.

Reputation—a little history

Back in 1995—that's all of twenty-four years ago—my NatWest Securities colleague traded the very first contract for difference (CFD) for the then-number two derivatives sales trading desk in UK. A year later, we made it to number one in equity derivatives brokerage and stayed there for a couple of years.

The CFD came into being a little earlier on single equities

quite simply to avoid stamp duty; quite a heavy tax payable immediately on purchasing quotes securities.

Some years later, after I had sold millions of these to my clients, I was working on a derivative desk at HSBC investment bank on Queen St., London, and I wanted to trade some myself. I went home to Fulham to my clunky, wired Ethernet connection and on one restless, balmy summer night, I hit on my answers: I wanted to trade UK stocks but outside these shores. I alighted soon upon Saxobank of Denmark.

How the world and reputations do swing. I read in a q3 (2017) edition of *The Economist* that Saxo's just been bought, by a—yes, you have guessed it—Chinese car manufacturer!

My point is, harking back to the Bloodhound land speed record story, reputation (like that of Saxobank) is fragile. I shall be tracking the bank under its new ownership to see whether reputation is compromised or (as is often the case) it is cautiously taught the Chinese way and keeps its "good looks" intact. Honour in China counts for a lot. If one can be relied upon, a lifelong, positive and self-reinforcing reputation may be in front of you. As ever though, and this is a mantra for this book: *"Be very careful."*

What implications do eerie activities like those of recent times in equity markets have on reputation risk management? Saxo was reckless in non-core areas of its business. It could afford to be so, ensuring its margins on cost and sales price differential were impressive, and "hedged" its already cautiously managed VAR[25] exposure arising from relatively feeble CFD exposure (by US standards anyhow).

Brand and risks vary inordinately between these two major

---

[25] VAR—value at risk.

industries. How can the two prance down the aisle in love (possible) and continue harmoniously indefinitely (less likely). One is staid and tangibly old-fashioned (cars) and the other is intangible yet alluring; banks' and insurance companies' returns on capital employment are irresistibly high[26]. Cars, on the other hand, have very lofty barriers to entry and spend all their reserves and returns on advertising and marketing. Many of the automotive sector companies own finance arms now, charging highly exorbitant APRs[27]. This is likely creative accounting under another guise. They are hedging their cash flows in cars (which are *very* slow) against the "upfront" payments and cash flow generated by financing deals, which are smaller yet regular and lucrative. Arguably, this is an efficient and profitable way to manage a risky portfolio.

With the advent of internet, cars' supply chains have migrated online but the relative fall in prices experienced by makers hasn't yet crossed the line to benefit consumers.

Why is this? In a word, greed (or more politely, avarice). It is very similar in the petroleum retail market: when oil prices in the North Sea and Texas spike (crude oil), the petrol prices race upward. When OPEC floods the market with the black stuff and the crude price collapses, the petrol prices will slide away *extremely* slowly—nothing like a similar percentage fall. Again, multinational greed accounts for this price behaviour. In their defence, petrol stations do have high-ish barriers to entry and fixed maintenance costs; even so, the driver is still a net loser.

For the same reason, that 22% ROCE (return on capital employed) has never translated to consumers becoming

---

[26] In 2007, they were "sky high" and came down dramatically in the crisis. Now they are creeping back to 2007 levels once more.

[27] APR—Average percentage rates of interest.

better off. Financial services' consumers are consistently arbitraged[28] by investment banks, insurers and retail financiers alike. This in plain English means that they buy at prices that are lofty when markets are buoyant and sell in semi-panic mode when prices are coming off (going downward). While the providers buy low and sell on high, so the dominant consumer behaviour is buy high and either hold and lose (to long-term inflation) or sell at absolutely lower levels—they've been had!

This inequality-creating trend is human-nature determined. Avarice overrides all.

Now let us turn our attention to marketing and the intangibles that determine where and why risks occur; invariably attributable to emotional intelligence and intellectual property.

---

[28] *The providers deliberately advertise and market more aggressively during times of asset bubbles in order to draw more punters in. At lower asset prices in less bubbly markets, banks go quiet or at least vanish into the shadows. Again questionable human behaviours come to the fore.

CHAPTER 3

Marketing Risk: IP (intellectual property) and EQ (emotional intelligence)

THE KEY ASSETS at risk and how you can manage them in a world where "assets tangible" have been superseded.

Distinctive Challenges

Arguably, the unique aspect of marketing is that, to be exceptional, it has to play straight into human feelings, senses and emotions. As one watches, listens, feels or reads an experience, the senses should be stimulated, or rather, as many of them as possible should be.

The emotional intelligence of a population is a measure of how sensitive its people are to the "feelers" that third parties (unconsciously) extend. The extension of these tentacles is a vital part of human communication and is the internal sponge that (especially) a woman has to be able to absorb and then act upon. Women in most global northern populations form the majority of decision makers on most topics, finances, clothes, children and outings!

Action

The actions that marketers are looking for are engagement and ultimately purchase for consideration (usually monetary). Within social enterprise principles and with my own doctoral study in mind[29], I recall a medium of exchange called the Brixton pound (B£). I am conversant these days with Bitcoin and Ethereum to name two of the cryptocurrencies. The new considerations are no less valuable or meaningful than the folding stuff! The "fact" that cash is more valuable is only a perceived truth; perception does not equal reality in this case.

Nowadays, in my own humblest opinion, too many people inhabit social media for the majority of their waking hours. They literally live out their lives online. This has a number of unintended consequences, the chief of which is a distinct lack of interaction in and with the ***real world, its organisations and its people.***

When real people implement the above action(s), this sequence of events not only includes the transactional (buying something) but it also encompasses what you say about the product or service and thus who you tell it or sell it to. Word of mouth remains the number one advocacy tool. Most of any product's sales are accounted for in this way; nearly all research has always shown this.

---

[29] My PhD into Social Entrepreneurship in the UK was terminated early due to the field research client (ETEC) in East Sunderland going into administration.

Initiation—the Creatives

The content of a marketing proposition is product and quality centric. The features have to be pronounced and described. The way the messages are conveyed are peripatetic; they vary enormously from country to country and between the continents. The risks are those of intellectual property containment: controlled sharing of data, information harnessing and then translating this into a b2c (business to consumer) experience.

Risks

Misdirection—segmentation is not accurate and slips past the best customers.

Inappropriate wording, phraseology and gimmicks.

Word-of-mouth should be transmitted electronically and through web marketing but instead is trampled underfoot of muddy boots in pamphlet form and in discarded white prepaid envelopes, often with throwaway pens. Most of all this enters paper recycling or landfill.

Channels: Missed opportunities—concerts, parties, conferences and seminars—at which presence should have been ensured but was not. Due to said mobile devices, young people have not taken to carrying business cards; more missed opportunities to make an impression.

This deficiency in marketing is all a function of how diligent and hard-working the marketer is. If (s)he works hard and ensures a team member's attendance at all seminars and all events like those mentioned above, pipelines will warm up and demonstrate decent conversion rates.

Distribution Processes

The trouble with doing business in 2018-2019 is that nigh everything is filtering direct into the public domain. There were, back in the nineties and the noughties, multiple thousands of agencies underneath the WPP and Publicis giants that were peddling "key messages" for products and services in the Internet epoch. Now that Mr Martin Sorrell has departed WPP under something of a cloud, this structure for the whole industry has started to re-fragment. Especially relevant is the fact that Sorrell is starting his own venture capital company, having already raised £100m from "friendly" warm investors.

The risks created by the "cloud" and the social media's public domain are numerous and tricky to manage. The management of a brand's "core" in the classic "apple" formation is still holding true[30]. There have to be synergies across strands and management of the core message. Now, in 2017, the western economies are all dominated by a few tech-centric companies; Apple peddles exceptional product, Amazon peddles exceptional retail experience. Google searches far and wide in an all-encompassing way and Facebook allows most of us who choose its route to share personal, experiential moments—incorporating graphics, cameras, videos, abuse[31] and analysis.

As Dell, Inc. had discovered by the time it took all of its outsourcing back in-house, the delegation of a) a marketing product gimmick and b) its delivery, to third parties has

---

[30] The core apple of marketing (this could but does not refer to Apple Inc) rather originates from MBA learning. The segmentation of the market place using "slices of the apple" as the metaphor.

[31] By the date read, this will turn into full-blown outrage of customers in the public domain; invasion of private space. Over-reach.

considerable hazardous risks attached. The core, necessary competence is *project management* in these instances; though not technically driven, it has to be technically competent and cognisant.

Outputs

The local newspapers, the fliers and the national TV slots are gradually being superseded by many things digital. The audience is more transient and more impulsive. There is research to be done and purchasing decisions to be arrived at, but the in-depth expertise and research that used to be the case no longer (sadly) pervade the process. This must change over time as the new output dynamic establishes itself as an emerging paradigm.

Impact

Everything marketing starts and finishes with the customer. The risk is that people think it lies with how much she spends, but NO, it all starts and finishes with how they feel as they're walking in for the first time: the eye contact you make with them, how you make them feel, and who they then went on to share these experiences with. The word of mouth factor is the big risk; in a positive way it is an opportunity that can be seized upon. As a threat, it is a moment of truth that you've em . . . screwed up—large.

This is the tenuous nature of that moment of truth; it is make or break in a jiffy for you and all other customers. If you have under- or mis-delivered, get out there and put it right instantly. Take a personal interest and be accountable for fixing it and seeing it through. Take a moment to say please and thank you and let the accompanying adults and children know how much you care. Do not risk bad word of mouth. Be circumspect about competitors—are they on site, nearby or waiting to pounce? There may even be a devious mystery shopper; this is big business now. Keep your antennae up at all times.

Other Sectors—A Short Exploration

Charities

Since they are now an embedded part of many major UK high streets, it is worth exploring the world of the third sector, or charitable organisations as they are more widely known. My reasoning is that, in charities, marketing is integral to the fundraising effort, which spreads to all functions within the service and delivery of any charity.

How they derive their income and how this is concentrated can affect the solvency and existence of a charity, and the marketing risks attendant can teach us a lot due to their high importance both within and to the world outside.

In funding terms, 49%[32] of income was derived from governmental contracts in 2001. By 2015, in a major way under Messrs Blair and Brown in the UK, this figure (shockingly, in my opinion) had moved up to 81%. For solvency, and with the benefit of "austerity Britain" hindsight, this is a huge concentration risk. This alert was repeated many times by me on my sojourn as a director through the "third" sector from 2002 to 2013. The dependency risk was and is ever high. Charities, even now—a full ten years after the crash of 2007-2008—continue to struggle with maintaining services that they are contracted to deliver on thinner budgets, but have **zero**

---

[32] Charities Commission Statistics 2002

working capital. In practical terms (and one can see this on the High Street), charities are increasingly using untrained and unpaid volunteers. Managing these (mostly) saintly people is no mean feat; it is rather an art form. This means against slimmer resources and falling municipal contracting income, they are borrowing in the form of punitive bank overdraft facilities. The borrowing is from the same finance establishments that nearly sunk the system back in 2008 and 2009; Lloyds (needless to say, TSB), Royal Bank of Scotland, Halifax and Bank of Scotland, all of which received bailout funding in the multiple £billions.

On a similar theme, in the same sector in 1982, 48% of income in American charities was accounted for by product and services sales. By 2013, this had moved up to 56%. This is another concentration of risk since the organisations are relying upon a consumer-driven economy, continuing, in what is now with rising US interest rates, a more hostile fiscal environment. Even short blips upward in the level of interest rate can and will likely have a devastating effect on (our) debt-laden service users. In the US, due to the sector being in absolute terms much larger, this "trend" is a little worrying since the consumers' purses are also shrinking or being squeezed.

One must remember that these two concentration risks are marketing risks since they both put the onus on marketing and fundraising units to raise their game in the squeezed environment. Work-life balance for many a fundraising team has gone out of sync. Mental health problems are seen much more obviously in wider society as more people feel an inner and external pressure to perform, or invest much more time in work, in order just to "stand still" in terms of basic necessities' provision. Food banks, themselves time- and resource-pressured charitable services, are saving more previously comfortably off consumers than ever before. They are now a feature, like the charity shops that preceded them, of almost all UK high streets.

Intellectual Property

No matter what social media distribution channel one follows—the newspapers, the printed journals, the Facebook platform, the network that is LinkedIn or indeed Twitter—you will not have failed to notice the following: #BigData.

Your personal and professional data, you can still call it yours when it's disbursed albeit in a fragmented way all over cyberspace. Anyone under the age of thirty, for sake of argument, for reasons of nature as well as time pressure, has not been as guarded and even circumspect as they perhaps should have been, especially since the turn of the millennium.

Those two years (1999-2000) were a watershed for the fault lines of digital data; the millennium bug where a computer, for reasons of human error (we were told), may recognise two zeros (00) on a date "string" as 1900 instead of the landmark 2000.

Many people in private and public sectors alike were rightly spooked and rushed out to hire battalions of software/hardware engineers and (high level, highly paid) "consultants" to check out their networks and internal interfaces, and their entire system infrastructure, inside and out, internally, internationally as well as externally.

In the anti-climactic event, nothing, or rather not very much at all happened. False alarm. However, for the Generation Ys, this was as mentioned a landmark since one humongous sector of the economy, IT (information technology), hadn't gone wrong.

The trust that has carried my eldest daughter's generation forward was contagious; the entire under-sixties population of the globe now puts its diary, its reminders and its personal and professional data online, in "the cloud" and on the hard drives of laptops, iPhones and Androids alike. The level of exposure that this creates for two-thirds of the world by demographics is simply, straightforwardly potentially catastrophic. Worrying times indeed.

Social Media

According to a recent article in a respected newspaper, anything that an adult does not understand on the internet is dubbed social media. Many adults indulging in parenting are not engrossed in social media and apps as the kids know them; they're on their own "boooorrring" Facebook page or in a group on the FB app discussing a teedddiiioouuss recipe for this evening's dinner.

The kids are where it's app: Whatsapp, Snapchat and Instagram. Activity on all three, due to their instant gratification imperative, has become frenzied; children are on them for longer periods of time daily than they're spending in school. In one respect, this is inevitable; in the same way my kid brother and I spent thirteen hours a day in the summer holidays kicking a rugby ball[33] around and playing on the swings and roundabouts, so now in 2019 do children pick up their smartphone.

On the other platforms, physically, physiologically and psychologically, it has simply got to have a detrimental effect on our youth and, more specifically, on their brains.

---

[33] With the exception of 1976; the weather was too poor for cricket!

Incidence of clinical depression in schools is shooting upwards exponentially; children are overly tired and stressed by all the screen-staring. Many don't know it, but many are aware, only too aware due to heightened anxiety leading to straying behaviour and self-harm. This could escalate to a more fully blown social crisis situation that it already is becoming.

One child, a fourteen-year-old from the Lylian Bayliss school in Kennington, South London, said, "I don't mind speaking to real people occasionally, just as long as I've got my phone near me"! The compromise of compromises!

Emotional Intelligence—The Part it Plays

Emotional intelligence is ageist, sexist and racist. It carefully ringfences the self; with watchful discretion, it chooses its friends, allies, favourites and customers ... even lovers, should it be in relaxation mode!

Outwardly, there are social filters that almost fully conceal the above innermost biases. This is where the "intelligence" part of the equation comes in. The right brain filters the ego into behaviours that demonstrate synergy and seek out calm chemistry between first people, then service and servitude and, last but not least, products and features.

All of this sits underneath one's cuticles, then picks and chooses strategic and tactical transactions in the manner of purchases and then guided interactions. These are all too often electronic interactions. I believe this non-human-interaction bias by young people is detrimental to their psychological wellbeing, but this discussion is for another book. Either way, the hazard and prevalence of risk is demonstrable here.

Risks are, as we shall see throughout this text, *physiological*. Behaviours can become overheated and overzealous. The flip side shows itself in indifference all the way down to precipitous depression; the latter states being still unacceptable in 2017, despite Mrs May's "action" on mental health. This is the phenomenon known as consumerization, the peer pressure to buy stuff and just keep buying.

CHAPTER 4

Catastrophe and Insurance: Worst-Case Scenarios

Catastrophe/Disaster

BUSINESSES HAVE BEEN able, in developed economies, to thoroughly model catastrophe for just over thirty years. Managers involved in product businesses should think about this seriously. It is possible in a high-risk area, for example, to model "hurricane, volcano or tsunami risk" using an eternity of possibilities in wind strength, tremor measurement and severity. Losses can be projected over a period of years and their frequency predicted, insurance taken out for protection or a senior decision taken to "do nothing". It is important first to identify the "critical plants" which, if shut down or destroyed, would destroy the entire business (or most of it) overnight. By concentrating on crucial areas, the decision lead time will be cut and the relevant risks can be quite quickly eliminated.

In relatively recent times (2010 Haiti earthquake, 2004 Asian tsunami), risk managers consider these events much more frequently than formerly, but the commercial difficulty comes in times of severe recession or, at the other end, in "booms" when companies make the mistake of either doing nothing at all or taking the "it will never happen to us" attitude.

The Credit Crunch 2007-2009

This crisis was precipitated by the collapse of liquidity in financial markets. Collateralised Debt Obligations, Security Obligations and Loan Obligations (CDOs, CDSs and CLOs) were "over the counter" instruments; crucially, these instruments were not traded on a transparent stock exchange[34].

Lehman Brothers was allowed to go into liquidation, which damaged market sentiment and underlying confidence. Sub-prime loans and mortgages went into freefall as liquidity seized up. People were simply unable to liquidate real estate which fell in value rapidly.

The Banks

By 2015 in the UK, Lloyds and TSB have been demerged whilst under government control; however it is maintaining its 43.4% equity stake. Royal Bank of Scotland is still reforming its investment banking arm, the value of the government's stake at £13.72bn is still much below the cost price of £45.5bn in 2009. In 2017, the government began discussion with an Abu Dhabi Wealth Fund but this has not resulted in a deal. The

---

[34] Conventional stock exchanges lend authenticity and transparency to companies that "list" and are quoted there. All of these "acronymous" instruments were OTC—over the counter—i.e. traded between banks and off exchange.

government lightened up its holding from 83% to 70% in May 2018 but 70% remains the main influence over the sluggish share price.

The eventual distribution to Lehman Brothers' creditors was $65bn; this has been painful for the marketplace whose bailed out insurance groups are still not out of the woods (AIG, Freddie, Fannie and Farmer Mac).

De-leveraging

This process involves increasing transaction margins substantially for funds, banks and individuals alike; thus tightening markets, withdrawing credit from the system. By 2015, the central banks were still continuing Quantitative Easing (QE) in large tranches; there is heightened risk for all if any Western government raises interest rates. The Euro currency remains under considerable threat, especially with the 2019 delays and chaos caused by Brexit.

Quantitative Easing

Printing money (including Euros) continues at pace at the ECB[35], the Bank of England and to a lesser extent at the US's Federal Reserve. Large corporates which have significant debt issuance remain under threat. In 2015, nervousness and market volatility remained a feature. These conditions persist in 2019.

---

[35] The ECB, European Central Bank has indicated to markets its intention to "retire" QE by the end of 2019.

Stop Press Emerging Themes and Thinking—New Processes, New Derivatives, Better Toolkit

The end of QE in the US and UK has been implemented and the ECB ceased in its Autumn 2018 cycle. This was a landmark moment when the central banks halted the kicking into the long grass and began fiscal tightening of interest rates. The smallest moves upwards may now rebound on borrowers; they are still too highly geared for the assets that they have in reserve (very few in most cases). President Trump is volatile. In mid August 2019 he brings great pressure on the Federal Reserve to lower interest rates; simultaneously he back-tracks on Twitter on the US/ Sino tariff conflict. Uncertainty reigns.

Brand and Reputation Risk

"Loss of reputation" has become a more commonplace fear among CEOs since the 1990s' advent of the super brand and the reinforcement of high risk that comes from interplay between customers on the worldwide web. Brands can be destroyed in a short "blogging" exchange between customers. By informally communicating (and inadvertently publishing) in this way, customers can destroy or uncover hidden pricing differentials and then damage an organisation's viability.

Rigorous Analysis

JP Morgan, one of the pioneers since 1992 of modern risk analysis techniques, recommends the following approach to the management of risk:

1. Appreciate that there can be *no return without risk*.
2. Understand and be transparent about risk; avoid risks that you cannot or do not understand.

3. Gain experience; a new model will never substitute for an experienced risk manager.
4. Always know what the assumptions are and continuously question them.
5. Encourage a culture where risks are aired openly; communication is vital.
6. Diversify risks, avoid concentration.
7. Be consistent and rigorous, showing discipline in your risk methodology.
8. Use common sense; do not spend infinite time striving for perfection.
9. Get to a "RiskGrade"; assess the true returns of your business by accurately measuring all the risks associated with them.[36]

Value at Risk (VaR)

VaR, as the name suggests, has an intrinsic defensive quality. It asks what value will be protected by removing risk. A developing theme in the risk management industry is "what value will be created by retaining risk". The CEO and board now have the power to decide the positioning of the firm's risk policy and with this relatively recent accountability may come a more defensive, cautious approach.

> Enterprise value = Future cash flows + Growth opportunities + latent value

---

[36] Source: http://www.riskmetrics.com. Sold off as a self-sustaining risk measurement consultancy company in 1996 by JP Morgan.

Cost of Capital

(tangible assets) + (premium value) + latent value

Risks associated with this equation are as follows:

Market risk interest rates, FX and commodity prices

Hazard risk—physical damage liabilities, commercial interruption

Operational risk—managed within sectors and regions

Strategic risk—"beyond derivatives".

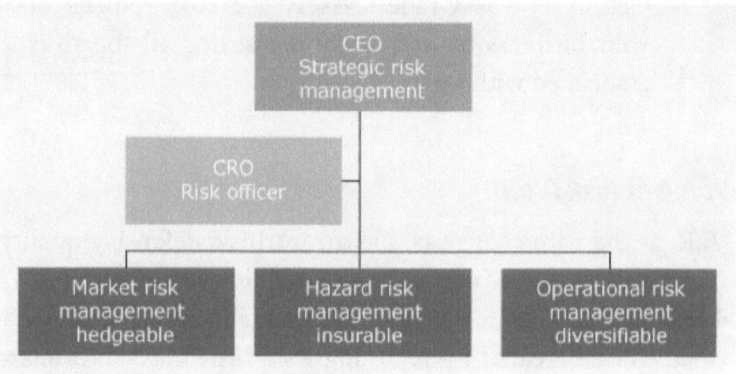

Fig. 3: The role of the Chief Risk Official

In larger organisations, this structure would nicely encapsulate where modern thinking has now come; does your company have any such clear division of risk responsibility? This may help you and your company refresh the structure around some anticipative thinking.

Case Study—Systemic Risk (2007-2015)

It is no exaggeration to suggest that since 2007 the developed economies (with one or two exceptions, including Canada) have been in financial and, to an extent, moral crisis. In these environments, individuals and countries have been taking outrageous risks almost unnoticed. Examples are given later in this case study.

Since the last amendment to this book, there have been some notable publications by professionals in the finance and risk sectors, of which notice should be taken. First, the *Financial Times* Business Book of the Year 2014 was *Capital in the Twenty-First Century* by Thomas Picketty of the Paris School of Economics. Second, *Antifragile* (2012), by Nassim Nicholas Taleb, a Lebanese-born author and risk analyst, who, until 2004 was also a financial options trader.

Both authors and titles have one common quality: pragmatism. Picketty took fourteen years to complete the former; it is an insightful examination of how an "endless inegalitarian spiral" is taking root across the globe. This "stirs discontent and undermines democratic values" with the risks being "potentially terrifying". Picketty's analysis is thorough, as thorough as Marx and Engels were. He concludes that the answer to the global distribution crisis (inequality and "the race to the bottom") which exacerbates the exploitation of labour, is the imposition of a progressive tax that (pro)actively redistributes income from the wealthiest down to the poorest. The other alternative is a *Tobin*[37] tax, something I think will be

---

[37] The Tobin tax was originally defined as a tax on all spot conversions of one currency into another. Over the years (as most deficits have grown) the tax could be levied in EVERY SINGLE transaction tax in financial services from share purchases and

preferable as it penalises ruthlessly those who can afford it the most.

Not for the first time, Europe's lesser powers are in deep trouble. For instance, in January 2015 in Greece, a coalition of extreme left and extreme right parties was voted into power after vowing to aggressively seek forgiveness of much of its national debt. Youth unemployment in the indebted European countries is up to 40%. Reverting to Picketty, "the past is devouring the future" due to the level of negative assets owed by the sovereign states.

To examine some of the data given to us by Picketty is useful. As the average rate of return on (largely inherited) capital exceeds the percentage rate of economic growth, one can see this "cannibalization" at work. Reiterating the leading paragraph of this case study here are highlighted three examples with neither complexity nor jargon.

a. Witness how English entrepreneur Mike Ashley of Sports Direct Ltd and Newcastle United has extremely quickly and with precision taken control of much of Rangers FC in Glasgow, Scotland. He now has a lien (security) over the Murray Park Training Ground and controls 75% of the shares of Rangers Retail Ltd. This is a strategic fit with the Sports Direct chain and has an appealing historic return on capital. Fans and a fierce culture tend to underpin leading Football

---

sales, as well as—the tiniest tax—on cash withdrawals. It is arguable that the tax generated would be a massive "take" for the world's governments—then occasioning the opportunity to start aid programmes and training in ICT for example for the poorest nations.

Clubs. On the high street, he has been linked (2019) with Debenhams which is all but in administration.

b. Whilst the Western world has been licking wounds and preparing for crucial elections, Russia has annexed Crimea and waged war aggressively in Ukraine

c. Under corporate governance regimes in the western world, "Top managers (1980 -2014) have had the power to set their own remuneration"; this exacerbates inequality and gives rise to more of the aforementioned (social) risks.

Above, (b) and (c) demonstrate how individuals and nation-states see risks as opportunities; (c) is enshrined in corporate governance legislation—see *resources* section in **Appendices**.

Also, early in 2015, Swiss government officials lifted the Swiss franc's cap against the €uro. This hit the SMI Index (the Swiss Stock Market) hard as the currency appreciated by 30% *in minutes*. The European bond yields fell across the board, oil (weakened by Saudi oversupply) fell further and gold once again rose in heavy trading; a hallmark of the markets' symptoms of nervousness: the rush to a safer haven. By August 2019, silver had risen to highs too; as Merryn Somerset-Webb said in her *Financial Times* column, "investing is more about geopolitics now than it has been for a long time". The next three decades is going to be much different from the last, which is going to make investing much more complicated.

Other recommended reading that is not so recent: Dan Gardner's pithy *Risk* (2010) and Nobel Memorial Prize Winner Joseph E. Stiglitz's *The Price of Inequality;* Richard Thaler and Cass Sunstein's *Nudge* which shows readers how governments can and have become "choice architects" under neo-liberal democracies.

Stiglitz made the following points April 21, 2009 in a keynote speech. "We have a system which created risk and misallocated capital with high transaction costs. Since 2009, have things changed? There have been a few minor corrections, but overall, markets have been stable at the higher levels. There are no outstanding bubbles in financial indices (the S&P in US is at relative peaks in recent weeks however, investing has indeed become complex), but the UK property market is "simmering underneath". As I write (August 2019), the London property market is steadily sliding off; were this proven to be precipitous, we should all be concerned. Indeed we will, or at least our offspring definitely will.

In the US, Elizabeth Warren in 2007 recommended a Financial Product Safety Commission, which has (to the author's knowledge) not come into being in the US or globally. This could be seen (and was) as a knee-jerk reaction to sub-prime crises but was necessary nonetheless. This underlines how self-regulation in financial markets never works; individual material thirst is immortal down the generations.

Here is a quote from J.Stiglitz's address: "We have too big a financial sector". The question, nearly six years on, is "Have we learnt our lesson"? An examination of bank share market capitalization is insufficient; it is the bankers' influence and inordinately powerful and persistent lobbying that really counts.

As Edward Liddy said, AIG[38] (to name but one bailed-out organisation) was "too complex, too unwieldy, and too opaque to function as one entity". Citi and AIG both received huge

---

[38] AIG—American Insurance Group Inc

subsidies under TARP[39]. Many of Stiglitz's recommendations fell on deaf ears; they should not have.

Jeffrey Sachs, among others, wrote about the opportunity for the banks to game the system. They went ahead; transferred debts do not disappear, hence the US deficit growth. This remains a significant systemic risk which may expand as economic activity slows in China, where US assets depreciate on the Chinese balance sheet. Levels of transparency now make little difference.

On regulations and regulatory enforcement of our large commercial and investment banks, Stiglitz said, "This is what has to be fixed". In 2015, expert commentators remain unconvinced that things have altered. Stiglitz makes reference to the Corporate Welfare State; clearly, he is referring to banks and reinsurers as AIG is mentioned in the transcript.

This macro case study affects us all. What it means to SMEs[40] and blue chips alike (excepting bail-out recipients) is lower growth and more expensive credit terms which will again fuel inequality on all time horizons: short, medium and long. There are some green shoots in this mist. Metro Bank is fresh and strong as a new entrant to the banking sector, as is First Utility in the utilities sector. Considerably more similar news is desirable; it remains to be seen whether 2015-2022 has the suitable climate for it.

Following the "polluter pays" principle, Stiglitz (like Picketty later) recommends a wealth tax that is progressive. He only recommended the tax be on "bailed-out banks' profits". Eight years on, this seems like a pipe dream. It requires more aggressive integration in Europe (unlikely in view of Greece

---

[39] TARP—Troubled assets relief program

[40] SMEs—Small and Medium sized Entities

and others) and cross-nation political harmony (rarely evident since *1700*).

There are two quandaries that linger with us:

- The development of a shadow banking system—what and where next for crowd-funding and peer to peer(P2P) lending? This is strengthening as quickly as ever as blockchain and fintech take hold.
- That a relatively small investment in (U.S.) election campaign contributions by financial, insurance and real estate firms—estimated at c.$5bn over a decade—has succeeded in transferring losses well in excess of US$1 trillion from the private sector to the public (onto Governments' balance sheets) without asking. This figure is still on the rise, specifically in the US and UK and more generally in the Eurozone.

CHAPTER 5

Star Talent Risk: The Exposure to their Departure

Retaining Your best Talent in a Universal "gig economy" Environment

As the saying goes, nobody is indispensable. But is this true? Does it hold fast if one-third of a three-man team in the City of London, for example, leaves for pastures new and a mega-golden "hello"?

In a market where talent is rare and aggressively coveted and bid for, there is a cogent argument to say that good people should be harnessed in a solid and comfortable team environment. True teamwork is something I have experienced and fundamentally it involves doing *everything* with and for the team, except sleeping of course. We[41] must have excelled since we were number one derivatives sales team three years on the run. There are important parallels with elite sports people here; they crave selfishness and self-centredness yet are capable of being team players if treated well.

---

[41] NatWest Securities UK Equity Derivatives Team Number One rated 1992-1995

In the hard, bloody and fast environs of financial services, loyalty is at a premium. If you discover a team ethos that is inhabited and practiced by people you like (and usefully too, who like you), this must be cherished and cannot be "priced up" as the City of London phrase goes.

The work and life pressures that you endure in your twenties and thirties shape your mood and your temperament in the short run. Over the longer term they shape your lifestyle and your quality of life deep into retirement, so it is advisable to pay attention to them and make of them the best that you possibly can.

High performance finance teams can brim over (by dint of what they do) with technocrats who stare deep into the spreadsheet (and love to) all day, every day. To retain very good people, you may have to—regularly in many financial services instances—ensure that these people feel appreciated. Give praise often, provided it is due. This reinforces esteem and earns reciprocity to the benefit of you and other team members. These are factors in high-performance team-building—wanting success and feeling needed in terms of one's technical and professional contribution.

Carrot or Stick?

As harsh as this may sound, with high performance—think 1990s treble-winning team Manchester United—the stick works well.

Sir Alex Ferguson is (I think, I cannot bring myself to read his autobiography) a self-confessed bully and harassment machine. It took David Beckham[42] a significant number of years

---

[42] Mr Beckham recently expressed his displeasure at lack of a

to stand up to him and the only day he did (after Fergie had injured him with a football boot missile), it marked his last few hours at Manchester United. Oh dear, how sad, never mind!

With arch and competent exponents of rugby union, the carrot I believe works better than the stick. Sir Clive Woodward, in his best seller on leadership, *Winning*, speaks of getting the players everything they need in order to support utter concentration upon their own performance. Clive carried this out to the letter with his evolving squad during 1997-2003, culminating in a World Cup victory in November 2003. He majored on elimination of "negative energy" from his squad. The famous case here was the dropping of Richard Cockerill, one of his best players, as he was consistently dropped and ignored. Woodward drew heavily on Yehuda Shinar's *Think Like a Winner*, (2007), although I think that he mistakenly placed too much emphasis on financial incentives for elite sportsmen. Sir Steve Redgrave is not a wealthy or high profile man; he was the very best though.

Then—and there's a lesson here—he (Clive Woodward) took spoiling the players to a whole new level with the 2005 British Lions tour of New Zealand; his aging England greats were, unfortunately for all concerned, past their best. But Clive managed to spend £10m of Rugby Football Union's (RFU)[43] money and his players were asked to focus on their rugby

---

Knighthood—Dear QEII, please continue to refuse to reward failure—both in winning or even qualifying for major tournaments as well as failing to win World Cup hosting bids to FIFA.

[43] By this time, Sir Clive had already been persona non-grata, yet he managed to fund raise from the Union because somewhere within himself and the Union, there lurked a belief that 2003 success could be repeated.

and *nothing* else. This entailed heavy curfews and denial of family company to the detriment (it turned out) of the team's performance. Alistair Campbell even went along to deal with spin!

The spoiling element bred an unhealthy dependency culture and this was manifest in some shoddy behaviour from a Mr Matt Dawson, who "told all" about training camp disharmony and how the management had become over-ambitious and overpowering.

Success, Continued

In the third quarter of 2017, I was taken aback to see an autobiography out by England elite rugby performance director Rob Andrew. Once a highly competent stand-off, Mr Andrew was in over his head when he assumed this crucial role in England rugby. As elite performance director, he was responsible for the team's advancing its development and outperforming any side in its path. After losing in the South Africa-hosted final in 2007, Andrew was omitted from the 2011 Cup's management team to tour. How could this be? Well, he toured after a minor sulk and it transpired into a naïvely poor performance on the field, marred further by a drunken, silly display which took place, the majority of the time, off the pitch.

Martin Johnson was gifted himself on the field of play; a born leader, he was physically strong and had the work ethic of a leviathan. He led from the front at all times and often marshalled his forwards around him to reassure and emphasise tactics. Johnson was the chief factor in all the 2003 victories, even though Sir Clive Woodward would probably claim much of the credit. Andrew, from a risk management perspective, was the beneficiary of institutional inertia at the Rugby Football

Union. He was allowed to continue in the role after repeated failure as well as being "shuffled sideways" way after he was past his best. Thus is the difficulty of the management of talent; all good things can and do come to an end[44].

Managing gifted individuals is no picnic; sometimes the most talented individuals are the most difficult to manage and to look after. Given that competence does have to be managed and harnessed, a star salesperson is *the* most difficult; they are often loners and non-team players and they expect spectacular rewards, the best of the best for them. In order to prosper, this person can be relied upon to keep on delivering, but **you** (as their manager) have to keep on giving. To them (!) selfishness is a key trait. After long periods, this can all be a little wearing, but here are a few pointers:

- Delegate their hourly/ daily supervision to offload some of the man-to-man burden;
- Monitor their sales performance meticulously;
- Seek a third opinion in crucial decisions and at turning-points;
- Practice regular and informal reinforcement when praise is merited.

The Stick and the Service Industry

Now we are a service economy; it can, referring to the following chapter, be difficult to monitor and discipline staff whilst one

---

[44] Rob Andrew has since moved on from RFU duties; he is now the Chief Executive Officer of Sussex County Cricket Club—he was a Cambridge University Cricket blue to boot.

is on the road as a constant. With high performance, a pep talk late in the afternoon often won't work; they will not be switched on to "appraisal" at this time of the day.

The morning it has to be, and in plenty of time before start of play as it were. The "lessons from last week" starter is effective, pointing to what they did well and what can be improved with some work. If it is a situation where it all about the sales numbers, then highlight prevalent timings and flag for assistance. If they are "field sales", there may be points in the day or the week when the rep needs peer support; he may even ask for a midweek chat to catch up with you. For hipos [45], always take the time out; it will be worth the effort.

---

[45] Hipos—high performance individuals

CHAPTER 6

Virtual Staff Risks: Managing Remotely

STAFF ARE PEOPLE and "give them an inch and they will take a mile" should apply here. But by almost all accounts, it doesn't.

Research shows that aside from the one to four hours that are saved on commuting time, workers are consistently *more* productive (and profitable) if left alone, on the one hand, and given flexibility on the other.

Many women, for example, have caring duties for their children or alternately, for parents living with them or staying nearby. Many men are as proactive as fathers now, as they used to be as breadwinners. They get used to the time available and they are making up for lost time with their children. There is less work out there, even though money is extremely cheap and unemployment is statistically quoted as low. 4.5% looks magnificent, but zero hours contract staff with no job security and very few benefits are now the typical UK employees. Recent research has revealed that only 44% of American citizens will take a holiday break this year, citing money or lack thereof to be the reason.[46] I have personally gone from earning well over average wage (and my wife too) to well below the taxable threshold; a sizable precipitous drop that has been painful to endure, but it does help one to re-evaluate one's life priorities.

Loyalty

Uber is struggling as a technology application in the middle of a struggling transportation sector.

Sexism, racism, ageism, and exploitation, illegal working hours and sub-minimum wage remuneration have all been found to exist at Uber as its governance structure was exposed. Travis Kalanik, its founder, was forced over this period to resign. The company lost its London licence to practice. *Financial Times* journalist Brooke Masters wrote competently on the issues facing the company and its leadership; everything seemed to have been taken to the extreme in poor management. Kalanik was talented and still is but controlling such a whirlwind would be painful for any board, hence his undoing[47].

Despite regaining a London licence, which was abruptly deprived them last year, Uber struggles not only with its stars. Endless media coverage and employment research reports have shown that its workforce is exploited and its contractors abused. People working for Uber [48] are now globally dispersed and susceptible to other copycat taxi hails.

---

[46] *Financial Times* weekend 25/26th 2019.

[47] https://www.ft.com/content/e263f482-57fc-11e7-80b6-9bfa4c1f 83d2 Brooke Masters *Financial Times*. 23 June 2017.

[48] It was reported in 2019 that Uber has consumed $7.2bn in cash

Company Culture at Airbnb

Culture rules: if you set and you apply the rules of "how things get done around here" with underlying individual behaviours, the chances are there has to be an ethical collegiate culture like that of Airbnb. In the world dominated by small handfuls of multinationals, this space saving company is making a name for itself.

Brian Joseph Chesky, the internet entrepreneur who founded Airbnb, believes that the stronger the culture, the less corporate process a company needs. Corporate process is like a flowchart of the structure of activities that serve as a goal in order to provide great value and services to customers and to bring profit to the company.

The master of the "build" of ethos and culture as currently understood is the same Mr Chesky. Importantly, a few bullets about the personal values of the leader which are matched (at interviews) then passed across:

- the values to ensure business success: *customer service and delivery* and not a lot else;
- employee loyalty, longevity and enduring technical competence;
- ruling out bitchiness, the divulging of corporate information and bad behaviour per se on company hours;
- what are we here to do? e.g. save customers money and deliver excellent goods and services.

---

with zero profits thus far. Now that's what I call ineffective (economically) disruptive technology; please watch this space.

The third point rules out the creation or endurance of negative energy[49]; everyone <u>in</u> the team is working <u>for</u> the team.

Implementation of Such a Dream!

Talk the talk: put sharing and cooperating with regard to the customer experience at the centre of the business; share the customer data to enhance their enjoyment of what you have to offer.

Walk the walk: communicating with your ladies and gents is a must, find out a) what's bugging them and b) how'd they put things right.

Employees who work "on the road" day in and day out will appreciate the extra thought that has been put in.

---

[49] See *Winning* : Woodward, Sir Clive—see bibliography

CHAPTER 7

Fintech[50] Risk and Reward: An Opportunity like No Other

THE FINANCIAL WORLD and the incumbents will be rocked by fintech. Fintech's not new either... please read on.

It represents an opportunity like no other to take proactive control of your earnings, your future spends and savings, your pension and all your retained earnings until you retire—this is what fin-tech is, once you get your head around it.

The reason I'm writing this is to do just that, help you get your head around things, like:

- online insurance; the ease and advantage of "switching". Go Compare website, Moneysupermarket.com

---

[50] Fintech = the financial technologies that will be able to disintermediate the Fund Manager: Consumers, savers and investors alike will be able to become self-supporting when it comes to searching for homes for their hard-earned money.

and confused.com all facilitate better deals for the (global) consumer of financial products

- online banking—Do you remember Egg[51]?
- online trading and foreign exchange; remember T.D. Waterhouse[52]?
- online pension control.

Tiedermans. IG Index and remember CMC Deal 4 free?

Now we have more choice, but many of us are confused. We're offered (aggressively and proactively) online investment options, online pension fund management, and online annuities and endowments. Remember Equitable Life?

Presently members of the general public allow fund managers:

1. To independently (under a board of trustees) invest and spend their savings, and
2. To collaborate with partners and other investors in the absence of consent and to divest and relinquish control of funds without owners' consent.

This brings us to trading "on margin". The ability to buy or sell a security without paying or receiving the full price. Liquidity or lack thereof can affect volatility on assets and therefore affect the Implied Volatility on the price of the stock's

---

[51] Egg was born under the Prudential plc umbrella as one of the maiden Internet banks; it now trades under the Yorkshire Building Society's name as the market has (gradually) consolidated.

[52] TD Waterhouse—This brokerage traded under the Toronto Dominion name in Canada.

derivatives (these are most commonly known as futures or options).

These days, your single stock future is known as a contract for difference. One trades on (typically) 20% margin—if the stock costs a £, you pay the broker only 20p—the broker delivers to you or takes from you the full monetary difference between 100% of the price of the equity at the start of the contract and the price of the share at the close of business at the end of the contract. These contracts are known as CFDs. As I say, a leveraged "wager" on the price of a single security.

By the way, one can SELL the underlying equity as well. This is a bit more expensive as the stockbroker has to borrow the sold security in order to deliver it to the buyer. This process is (somewhat controversially) known as "short selling", i.e. selling the share in the hope of buying it back cheaper. Understand? I certainly hope so and have tried to simplify the terminology and the process as much as possible for you. It's just like selling a chair without owning it; you give 20p to the owner and he (the seller) then delivers it to you. If he has to borrow the chair, he charges you a nominal fee in order to facilitate the loan.

This can get tricky in thin (illiquid) markets as securities themselves become scarce and the broker has to "pay up" to borrow. But for most experienced traders, this wouldn't be a problem as long as the communication between front and back offices is functioning well.

Introduction

Technically, the following may occur as a result of fintech:

Millions of individuals take control of their own pension pots, pulling money away from "funds under management" by national and international asset management firms.

The governance of fund managers has to be on the lookout

for what may start a massive trend. This is the power of automation and, in time, passive funds themselves may come to automate their investment process; for example, "press 'buy automatically when the market comes off from current levels'" (say, 2.75%) at any time before (three months' time—for example).

Pension funds are ring-fenced by many corporate entities, but there is more than a sense out there that the majority of them are "under water". The shortfalls globally are in the low trillions here which, even if it were an overestimation, rings alarm bells at so many different levels. The pension deficits, even at the banks which are deep back into profits are IGNORING the perils of shortfall, after a full decade of tight margins yet improving profitability.

The funds under management are still rising, but tech-centric new entrants are creeping gently into the marketplace and fee structures, much to my and many other experts' relief, are under a reliable threat.

Old Mutual plc [53] is a South African insurer which took over an inter-dealer broker (GNI) in 2000. This is indicative of "risk profiling" since the former is very conservative and the latter is (was) crazily volatile. When the takeover was made, the markets lapped it up, yet later mass redundancies were made at GNI and almost all staff were lost in the quagmire that is fund management and financial services companies.

The very fact that the takeover was happening was an indication that p/e[54] ratios were too high and that the market

---

[53] 2001 2002 when I was employed by GNI Ltd, OM was dual quoted in the FTSE and on the South African Stock Exchange.

[54] P/E—price/earnings ratios. The price of the individual share as it relates to the profitability of the company.

reckoned (accurately) that the tortoise would overcome the hare.

Additionally, and with regard to managing star performers, the latter takes care of itself; high income earners manage themselves out of the business saving weak HR Managers a job/chore!

Fintech and the GDPR Imperative—Is it Imperative?

There has been a lot of clogging of old-fashioned mailboxes of late with banks alerting customers, making them aware (as blandly as they can) for the first time, of new, incoming General Data Protection Regulations. Data controllers and processors in short are the subject of more responsibilities thrust upon them. 2% of turnover or a straight €10million, whichever the higher, is the penalty for non-compliance. Serious. Given many firms' size, they can relegate this to a pure and simple cost of doing business and swallow resultant fines and penalties whole. This is not ideal from a customer perspective. WE want the market cleaned up; this way, by contrast, all the sleight of hand dirt remains. Please read on.

In the effective systems that I have seen, control of proprietary data has been handed to the customer and sensitivity of data is protected by encryption, pseudonymisation and data minimisation; a little technical, but you probably get my drift(?).

Cryptocurrency—A Revolution in the Making?

It is inevitable, given how money's history has remained the same for hundreds, arguably thousands of years, that a new era may sweep into the "unit of exchange" world. Intrinsic value vanished but there are still gold reserves that are taken seriously. Since money's conversion to token currencies, nothing's happened and this just might be about to change. The cryptocurrency has arrived with fanfare. Upwards of 202 initial coin offerings have been "floated" in the recent past and people have invested in excess of $3bn. These people must have envisaged a financial return. In some countries, ICOs (international Coin Offerings) have been banished[55].

Bitcoin stood alone in the public consciousness for some considerable time. Now Ethereum, among many others have swept onto the market and as I mentioned are backed by serious investors. As the pound went into freefall in the UK over Brexit, young people flashed their phones at the till to place orders/pay for goods. The upcoming generation see the coins in their pocket as mere commodities, a convenience for minimal consumption.

Blockchain

Blockchain, so the financial people would have us believe, is an "innovative" technology. It can do such wonderful things as transact a foreign currency deal and actually tell us how much the transaction is worth in both currencies; informing us instantly of how much we will be credited or debited. Like all finance transactions and with due regard to risk-taking, there is hidden cost: the *sizeable* spread[56].

Blockchain is the system that takes care of the processing, the chronological recording publicly of cryptocurrency

---

[55] Most notably in China

[56] The spread is the difference between the buy and the sell price quoted by a "market maker". This individual or company makes a profit of the differential between the two.

transactions which almost overnight are deluging ecommerce spheres of operation. To try to safeguard your data, how you collect it, protect it and share it, Blocksure OS seems to stand out. [57]

MifID[58] 2.0

MifID 2.0 IS MiFID II is a legislative framework instituted by the European Union to regulate financial markets in the bloc and improve protections for investors with the aim of restoring confidence in the industry after the financial crisis exposed weaknesses in the systems. The Europe-wide harmonisation of investment regulation, focused on the EU members of which Britain may not be one after 31 October 2019[59]. I am at a loss for words, given that thousands of compliance people have been hired to get their heads around this new wave and layer of control. The financial services sector is an overtly mollycoddled sector, looking after itself and a plethora of vested interests, as well and at the same time as making all the customers' lives that little bit more difficult. To this legislation, there are thirty-one country counterparts: that is the EU countries plus (Britain)[60], Iceland, Norway and Lichtenstein.

In the context of the US and its dominions, there is zero implication, but for the United Kingdom the 31/10/2019 will

---

[57] https://medium.com/blocksure/blocksure-os-proof-of-concept-17f4b04d1997

[58] MIFID—Market in Financial Instruments Directive

[59] Please see my appendix's papers on Brexit.

[60] Decision date is 10/31/19 but this is, in the words of PM Johnson, "touch & go"

overnight be out of sync with all its financial exchange-traded instrument settlement, not to mention the immense assets and liabilities present in the Over the Counter Markets for fixed income and equity derivatives, once my home ground.

The Lamfalussy Directive

This originated from the Baron Alexandre Lamfalussy; it is the preservation and continued enforcement of the European Union's passport (for financial products) introduced by the Investment Services Directive (ISD), the continuing harmonization-max of that grand European project which the former Governor of the Bank of England, Mervyn King, said was "at the heart of global disequilibrium"—always a phrase that stuck in my mind[61].

As of April 2018, the UK's House of Lords was seeking to part-reverse "Brexit" by passing a bill as an amendment to the Brexit bill which cancels trade tariffs on each-way trade with the twenty-seven other countries. This means that Britain stays in the customs union and that there will be zero borders in Ireland twixt north and south. Despite the relief in the fact of the latter, this is not what the people voted for, albeit with a 52% vs 48% vote (relatively slender majority).

> "Capitalism had flaws, democracy had an alarming tendency to undermine itself[62]."

---

[61] See Bibliography—*The End of Alchemy* by Mervyn King.
[62] Article on John Stuart Mill and philosophy *Economist* August 4 2018

Active versus passive Asset Management

Over the past two or three decades, there has been an unprecedented migration from active funds to passive in the global marketplace. For example, in 2016, passive funds attracted some $201bn of inflowing funds, whilst actively managed funds lost some $124bn. Costs in a "low return" environment are scrutinised with greater care and conservatism by the pension fund managers; these are quantum moves over the 365-day period.

This means firms like Vanguard are benefiting greatly in terms of FUM (funds under management) but Fidelity, the Boston giant with $303bn under management, has changed its fee-charging structure to reflect a reversal of trend, proof that people get a fairer deal if they choose to "get active" on their own behalf once more.

Investors, equitably for the first time in years (ever?) would pay for the performance and not for the *under*performance. Fund managers are usually remunerated on the amount of money in the cupboard and not on the performance in percentage terms of its appreciation[63].

Data tells us that passive is best since these funds outperformed the more expensive active funds; ironic but true. There has been an irresistible move into passive ETFs[64] (exchange traded funds), which mirror index performance

---

[63] There have been numerous commentators who remain critical of this anomaly. The structure of the industry which is "legacy" by its nature *rewards failure*.

[64] Exchange Traded Funds invest directly and in an exactly weighted fashion into stock indices using initially "futures" followed by purchasing the yield-bearing equities

exactly, and away from active investment (for example, into tobacco as against into airline stocks).

One counter argument to fintech is fronted by time. One must be blessed with many hours in order to be able to efficiently and effectively manage a pension pot. Plus, when you own all the assets yourself, this makes the process ever more taxing, literally and metaphorically. With the invention of instruments such as derivatives and vehicles such as ETFs[65], the time necessary to have the necessary commensurate understanding has shortened.

Trading Online

IG Index made its name in a field with which back in the nineties I was to become all too familiar: the contract for difference (CFD).

From there, the company diversified into index contracts and then into spread betting in matters of business and sport. They hired in the relevant expertise and made great profit for two decades hence.

CMC Deal for Free: The IG success story was instigated in a panic move to compete against a broker selling product for zero cost. Lying beneath this ground-breaking move was the immutable fact that DFF[66] was building in an exorbitant bid-offer spread, thereby making a large trading profit instead of charging and yielding a small commission on each transaction.

The risks were mitigated by neighbours GNI, for whom I headed up product marketing in Europe for two years. They

---

[65] ETFs—Exchange Traded Funds: "Blocks" of equities that are traded and listed on Official Stock Exchanges.

[66] DFF—Deal For Free

used to sell the CFD to the client and buy the *exact shares* as a perfect hedge. As far as I'm aware, IG did not hedge a lot of their positions; they "ran them" or fancied the stock in a "naked" [67]position. The net positions were reported per compliance to the Stock Exchange and at that stage could be hedged in, for example, ADR[68] positions (American Depositary Receipts) in the US where the markets had just opened. The hedging had to be done in differing time zones encompassing the Far East.

PPI[69]—The Scandal That is Payment Protection Insurance Mis-selling

The PPI scandal requires a separate sub-section.

Banks (oh my!) have been misleading the common man since the year dot. The same is true in the 21st century when we are still clearing up after those practicing in the 1980s and 1990s (boom years). To explain: on overdrafts, loans and credit cards, the banks sold insurance policies (which customers never signed up for) protecting against worklessness (chiefly being made redundant by one's employers at short notice). Clearly, from data thus far available, they were allowed to get away with this for many years. The government, sensing that this one was going to run and run, and aware of the fact that lowly capitalised banks are still in charge of the global economy—

---

[67] "naked" denotes no hedge being undertaken by the salesperson / trader in question

[68] ADR—American Depository Receipts: The US version of a listed United Kingdom stock traded on exchange in the US whilst the UK market is closed overnight.

[69] PPI—Payment Protection Insurance—miss-selling insurance on financial retail products and credit cards.

that's the wrong way round by the way—has put an October 2019 time limit for claims. We have been told this is the final deadline for claims.

That is thirty-nine years approximately after the banks started to cheat us. Thirty-nine steps, as John Buchan would have put it! RBS NatWest, Barclays, HSBC, Lloyds TSB, Santander (formerly Abbey National Building Society Ltd) are the usual suspects. Rumour had it that LTSB was a crucial offender as was Halifax Building Society, which was merged into the entity before it divested TSB.

The calendar skips through those thirty-nine years and yes, they're at it again. Donor Assisted Funds (DAFs in America) are social enterprise vehicles that are supposed to be assisting US charities, yet the majority of the funds are flowing in to banking and fund management coffers rather than, as intended, being transferred to charities' good causes. Followed by car financing, as it's currently understood, apparently now a seller has to have a car FCA[70] Accreditation to facilitate the car purchase. *I do not think that anybody has spotted this one yet.* Whilst viewing Sky and NowTV predominant advertising space has been purchased at great expense by the car manufacturers; this applies too to the DIY specialists at Wickes and B&Q—their zero percent promises turn these products into loss leaders if credit tightens up. *I do not think that anybody has spotted this one yet either!*

In October 2017, I looked at the landscape and am yet shocked by what the banks still get away with. Overdraft exploitation adds insult to injury. Especially in the 1990s, when we were in a higher (much higher) and volatile interest rate

---

[70] FCA—The UK regulator known as the Financial Conduct Authority.

environment; in the first instance, the banks were charging way above "base rate" (usually already way above the London Interbank Offered rate—LIBOR), then adding a PPI surcharge. Yes, a bogus insurance policy. Another example that in any other industry would be sharp practice—but all the banks can and do freely practice it.

Annuities and Endowments

In the late 1990s, the first phase of this scandal came to light with a forthcoming period of much lower rates and the then-prevalence of inflation. Customers of the banks and their financial service provider partners in crime[71] would, with the proceeds of their payout, be UNABLE to pay off their future mortgage liabilities, by which time they would have retired and have no means of making up the shortfall. Conned again. These ineffective instruments were called with-profits endowments policies and one provider of such, Equitable Life, went bust. Others were accused of mis-selling! Needless to say, I was a victim myself with Allied Dunbar; still then part of a tobacco company (British American Tobacco—BATs). How ironic.

Annuities

Provided these are reduced (regularly and harshly) from projections made in the 1980s and are still active (live policies) in numbers, it remains uncertain that there will not be an annuities backlash to match those occurring with PPI, sooner

---

[71] The likes of the aforementioned Equitable Life and Allied Dunbar, previously owned by BAT (a cigarette maker!) and now by Zurich Financial, a Swiss financial behemoth.

too, rather than later. Endowments in the same form as they were sold (above) back in the nineteen eighties and nineties are no longer available in those dated and by definition dangerous forms/packages.

An annuity is very similar and as far as my experience dictates, have not been subject to material change across the life of the products, i.e. you don't normally get an annual downward revision that may have, at certain risky times, tempered your expectations. Hence, there is room for doubt that the "sale" to us was a clean and honest one. Déjà vu?

Do Hedgies Hedge?

Given the distribution of age along the trader curve, it depends what day of the week it is and how much alcohol was consumed the previous night or the same early morning! In my experience—and I hope that fifteen years, 1986-2001 seems considerable—if a trader buys or sells (from clients or from other traders) an evenly spread portfolio of stocks then she will sell the appropriately adjusted (weighted) number of futures, maybe with a small "punt"[72] embedded. If it is a bond, then she can delta hedge with appropriate equities or perhaps an interest rate futures contract or more. If it were to be a warrant, the corresponding delta on the security's equity and if it's a future, maybe an index weighted basket of stocks. Either way, it is possible to exactly "delta hedge" to immunise oneself against losses.

So, every exposure as demonstrated has a possible corresponding hedge, but whether she carries it through or not is,

---

[72] A one-way bet.

as I said, up to her[73] mood on the day. These "positions" that traders run are insured only by "word of mouth" and many an experienced "producer" has outfoxed an overloaded back office clerk; in Nick Leeson's case at Barings Bank in Asia, he was actually doing both jobs front and back.

What About Reinsurance?

For some micro-analysis on this, please read my case paper on the demise of Enron Inc (2003) at which time I was lecturing part-time on the subject of risk, uncertainty and chaos theory. My paper goes into case histories on the European giants Munich Re and Swiss Re, both intriguing stories in times of a) volatility jumps and b) catastrophe insurance jitters (9/11 related). They are still both current giants bearing a fair proportion of exposure to the pending commercial and mortgage lending crises (mark my words), as well as to the odd hurricane and typhoon, both of which have been ravaging the Americas and the West Indian countries in recent times. One can also purchase "weather derivatives", (insurance policies) for sporting events vulnerable to rain interruptions where income levels are severely affected. One such user is the Marylebone Cricket Club, which on any one test match day has approximately £2,700,000 at risk. That is some £10.8million as a Test Match runs for FOUR days rather than a single day…Ouch!

And . . . when to roll-over these risks? This will all be onerous for reinsurers; the time decay can be severe because the options can (or rather "have to") be very short dated and can expire at extremely short notice. Be aware of counterparty

---

[73] "Women Day Traders are on the Rise" https://www.howwetrade.com/women-day-traders-are-on-the-rise/

risk when trading over-the-counter (i.e. off exchange); it can be ruinous. The major day-to-day exponents of such practices are with arable farmers, whose large crops may perish under a c. 1976/2018 drought.

Behavioural Economics

In early October 2017, Richard Thaler won the Nobel Prize for Economics for his work on the behavioural side of things. This "science" has been more pithily known as "nudging people" after a book that Thaler wrote with co-author Cass Sunstein[74]. In a fit of, for once-sage, copycat behaviour, in 2011 David Cameron—who is answerable to 3 years of #Brexitshambles set up the UK government's nudge unit, which is still active. This was set up to nudge the population towards behaviours (eating habits, for example) that would be more beneficial to their health, their families' wellbeing and that of the country at large.

One of the striking facts about Nudge's UK history is that the unit recruited from Tony Blair's right-hand men, namely David Halpern. Loyalty or ethical behaviours do not figure with these expert consultants; they command considerable fees for which the public purse is paying and their effectiveness six years on is debateable.

Here is an extract from a recent *Huffington Post* article:

> "One of the most controversial pledges of (Theresa) May's general election campaign turned out to be something politicians did not know as much about as they thought. The Conservatives announced they would extend the right-to-buy to housing association tenants. After the

---

[74] Please see bibliography.

conservatives won a majority, the scheme attracted fewer applicants than expected, although the benefits of buying the house you lived in at a discount seemed obviously beneficial [75]*".*

This became another example of unimplemented policy; words, not deeds of the coalition and then-Tory-led government (2010–2015)

---

[75] *Huffington Post*, 17 October 2015.

CHAPTER 8

The Dangers of Over-Borrowing

Herein I'm all at 8s and 9s instead of 6s and 7s. Chapter 10 discusses stakeholders, more specifically stockholders, but the latter's valuations over the past decade have been pumped and fuelled by debt and leverage. Additionally, geopolitical risk is peaking; "Investing is more about geopolitics now than it has been for a long time"[76]. Central bankers, whose governments in many parts of the world are in serious debt, have collectively determined that low interest rates and quantitative easing are the way ahead. The trouble is there's a roadblock and that's reality.

Quantitative easing statistics: how much is the Federal Reserve (the Fed), European Central Bank and Bank of England programme worth collectively and individually?

QE has been happening ever since 2008 when the initial

---

[76] Merryn Somerset-Webb: "So many reasons to be fearful" *Financial Times* 24 August 2019.

signs of the credit crunch began and, according to Gavin Davis, the commentator (formerly Chief Economist) of Goldman Sachs, inflation and financial market distortions "are going to threaten stability". The "concerns" here outlined only started to worry authorities in 2017, a full ten years after the "crunch" began. A Federal Reserve tightening, followed by a Bank of England rated rise of 0.25% began in 2018. With (as ever) the US leading the way, Mark Carney as ever was the follower rather than the leader.

Even the BoJ (Bank of Japan) has joined the tightening party. The trouble with, as Davis describes it, "QE to infinity" is that it delays THE day of reckoning and increases its likely severity. Do please read on.

Debt is the driver of concern. The man in the street is addicted, the bank on the high street has sidled off into the shape of a cash machine and staff who tell us what they cannot do. In addition, the central bankers are all frantically trying to work out what to do next. It's their (Fed+ECB+BoE+BoJ) fault. Quoting Somerset-Webb again, "But the key message from Adam Smith-style talking has been more important: The next three decades will be different from the last three and that's going to make investing very complicated indeed".

The Minsky Moment

The investment managers on much of the global new north are fully invested at present, yet corporate entities (Apple, Amazon, Facebook, Netflix, Google, collectively known as the FAANGs) are long, vast tracts of ready, investable cash. Their generation of almost pure margin, after, in Amazon's case years to "foothold" its business model, is dominating *world consumption t*rade. This is game-changing; the world's supply and retailing chain has gone virtual. The "hub and spokes" click-and-deliver business model is not avant-garde, but rather the norm already.

This fact means that contagion <u>could be</u> about to hurt us noticeably more. The ease of borrow and spend in public, private and speculative marketplaces has taken asset market valuations to unprecedented levels.

As stated, *Financial Times* and *Money Week* journalist Merryn Somerset Webb, who also edits *Money Week*, is forever warning about this and Martin Wolf wrote a book on it[77].

As Paul McCully of Pimco said after the famous economist Hyman Minsky in 1998, by virtue of now-concerted action, the bankers periodically **set fire** to the economy.

Quantitative Easing (QE)

Minds must have been tested when politicians like Ed Balls—who is after a career in media[78] and is making a documentary entitled *Travels in Trumpland*, which is both engaging and fascinating for a spectator like me—Central Bank forgiveness and UK Chancellor Gordon Brown's determinism dictated that bankers sit round and calculate what to do next in the post-crisis environment of 2009. Make no mistake, there ensued a period of austerity, but it did not touch the sides regarding debt reduction. The elites thought about it, briefly, and concluded that this might be a step too far. Wrongly, in my opinion, and costly this will be.

In unison, they devised an alternative term for *printing cash*[79]. Markets were diving; banks were bailed out aplenty but

---

[77] See Bibliography *The Shifts and the Shocks* 2015.
[78] Balls now also lectures at Harvard in the USA.
[79] In 2007-2008, this phraseology was deemed a bit too alarmist.

the swish term "quantitative easing" sprang to Western central bankers' collective mind. This enabled, over a full decade, banks to repair balance sheets by boosting their "quantitative position" by gifting them free gilt-edged securities to falsely and dangerously bolster their balance sheets. This has been increasingly collateralised against each individual bank's loan book. According to many small and medium enterprises, this "bolstering" was not utilised to oil the wheels of working capital; rather, businesses were knowingly thrown to the wall whilst many of the bank's share prices embarked upon a recovery.

Systemically, the world is a strange and unstable place. The global media peddled by the West or the "global north" as it is known in anthropological circles, describes itself as the "rich world" or the "developed economies". Countries in Asia and Africa that do not run humongous trade deficits with the rest of the world and that have in some cases healthy, small trade surpluses are described as "the developing economies"; in many cases run by despots who maintain a healthy war-free environment. The West respects them, all bar America which wants—brazenly in some cases and secretly in others—to change the regime and introduce democracy. Hegemony in extremis, about which Noam Chomsky[80], the talented linguistics philosopher, has been writing in depth for some considerable time.

The world order to a greater, not lesser, extent needs what Gideon Rachman describes as "Easternization"[81]. China and others in the region and the wider world respect its "civilization"

---

[80] Please see Bibliography. *Who Rules the World: Reframings*. 2017.

[81] The main thrust of this book is around battles, wars and incursions involving Eastern domination but perhaps it will translate well

evolved, encouraged and garnered over thousands if not millions of years. The problem as the US sees it is that China is not a meritocracy but a contemptible communist state. Yet, to look at it another way, would you be more comfortable with the benign, non-inflammatory Xi Jinping or the irascible, irritable and forever volatile DJ Trump, whose narrative and tweets to and fro with North Korea and the Chinese are even optimistically cause for alarm?

America insists (as global leader in its own eyes) that North Korea's nuclear capability be contained and in an ideal world eliminated. Britain has said nothing; then again, Theresa May has done precisely nothing also. She is the passive, set-piece leader who is, like it or lump it, heading for the chop. The Trump summit with Kim Jong Un was inspirational and brave; tell the North Koreans what they want to hear and they are considering nuclear disarmament. Call Trump what you will but he, at least, is having a go, which is more than Barack Obama did in eight years. How does this all relate to risk? Read on.

Arguably, I say, all the instability in the world can be attributed to excesses of debt. The US owes the Chinese and Asian buyers of its debt trillions, literally. The world stands by and allows a debt-laden monster to be the global lender of last resort or, in another language, the reserve currency of choice to all those upcoming developing economies which one day soon will be seen to be and will actually be more powerful and influential.

The Asian Infrastructure Investment Bank (AIIB) should be watched closely since it will probably not move forward to

---

one day soon to what is actually happening in risk and finance—adoption of longer-term strategy must be the way forward.

displace (or try to) the International Monetary Fund and/or the World Bank.

The United Nations (UN) has addressed the launch of AIIB as having potential for "scaling up financing for sustainable development" for the concern of global economic governance. The capital of the bank is just over $100 billion, equivalent to 2/3 of the capital of the Asian Development Bank and about half that of the World Bank.[82] If it's 66% the size of the previously founded ADB and half the size of the World Bank by reserve capital, it must be coming up hard on the rails; its whip is silent and its speed hastening. Beware the United States of America.

The disturbing fact is that the Federal infrastructure in America threatens to shut down at regular intervals because the equivalent of the UK's civil servants are not happy signing up to print money ad-infinitum. These governmental shutdowns cause the majority of employees to survive unpaid, starving the US economy of valued consumers for periods. The nerves and harrowing uncertainty that must be bubbling within the officials under the surface is carefully guarded by the media power brokers; this is what is known as the delicate concealment of political and systemic risks. Gillian Tett of the *Financial Times* writes about this persistently and regularly; her two books *Fools' Gold* and *The Silo Effect* are to be recommended.

STOP PRESS 15 April 2019: President Trump received some bad news, too. A large majority of

---

[82] This short paragraph for succinct description has been lifted from notoriously reliable Wikipedia. If the numbers are correct, China's upcoming dominance is almost assured but I do not sense that it is actively being either tried or encouraged.

Americans think his claim to have lowered their taxes—and not just those of the rich and corporations—is fake news[83].

It was only ever a matter of time before something sensible happened with regard to the property market, in looking at the big picture. As reluctantly as I am as a Brexiteer, I turned a short while ago to Germany.

Angela Merkel has crept through her final stint as Chancellor, bidding to construct a three-way coalition between the CDU and two other parties. In the sensible weekend news at that time, the Bundesbank, the central bank of Germany, warned a largely renting population that it expects between a 15% and 30% correction in real estate markets, probably as a result of incremental rate increases. The European Central Bank is watching this closely but is perched on the sidelines, interestingly, in terms of "tightening".

Rhineland, et al's property prices have, I suspect, been pumped up by foreign investors and speculators in the form of inquisitive investors who thought that they were first to start taking advantage of an opportunity that entire European markets had missed. Interest rates in the country remain stable at lower levels so speculation fuelled by borrowing is still occurring. The "(cost of) carry trade", as it was known in Japan, is the same consumer and public sector tactic that got us to 2007-2008. Repetition seems inevitable. Assets' prices

---

[83] Kapur, Sahil, and Davison, Laura. "Trump gave most Americans a tax cut and they didn't notice". *Bloomberg* https://www.bloomberg.com/news/articles/2019-04-15/trump-gave-most-americans-a-tax-cut-and-they-didn-t-notice?cmpid=BBD041519_BIZ&utm_medium=email&utm_source=newsletter&utm_term=190415&utm_campaign=bloombergdaily—

from bonds (debt), equities, commodities (soft) and property are up at pre-crash high levels. There is, as one journalist phrased it, "an awful lot of bubble but little or no fizz". This growth feels like a benign tumour; alas, it could be more sinister.

Western or global north economies are highly susceptible to interest rate rises and Ms Janet Yellen and Mark Carney are, in the case of the former, gently raising them and, in the case of the latter, (very tentatively) just about to start. +0.25% in August 2018, the first rate rise for a decade.

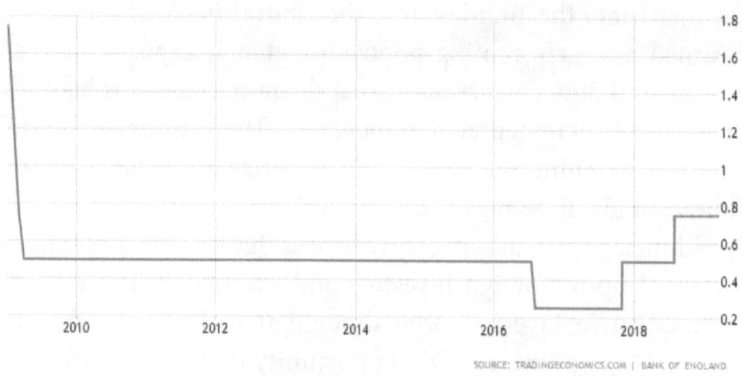

Figure 4.0—Graph of UK, Bank of England Interest Rates 2007-2019

Source: http://www.tradingeconomics.com 15th April 2019

At the lower end of debt bearers, where the APR is between 17% and 36% (and much much more), this will wipe out liquidity and confidence and spending power all at once. People will, I tentatively guarantee it, rather stay in the bath or the bedroom than go forth and spend on anything but basic food and toiletries. During what has been termed "the Great Recession", consumer demand did get choked off (in UK) by austerity measures implemented by Chancellor George Osborne.

With George departing to edit the London *Evening Standard* and advise Blackrock Asset Management after then Prime Minister Theresa May sacked him, Phillip Hammond has not been explicit about austere measures but he ran as tight a ship as he could. There was media hype around infrastructure spending when Mrs May began but, like most of her rhetoric, it proved hollow. Retailers are in trouble, including B&Q, Tesco, ToysRUs, John Lewis Partnership (incorporating the Waitrose brand), Matalan, and Poundland and Poundworld—this type of shop is wondering if one British pound is low enough for British consumers, which is worrisome.

Logic and a measure of brutal honesty dictates that this ends in a banking crisis preceded by a crunch on (the consumer)/on ALL credit. Liquidity in debt markets will embrace arid terrain. Equity markets will trek gently sideways and precipitously tumble. Hard commodities prices plus gold will spike on spot and long futures markets and European food prices will moderately soar. Brexit won't help us here in the UK.

Moderately soar is a cop out; they'll be higher and then will be ramped upward by youthful avaricious speculators. There may well be plenty of those during forthcoming uncertain times.

Somewhat on the flip side of the coinage, Chinese government debt has spiked of late. The same principles of Western inequality prevail; the rich are running up needless overdrafts and loans and the middle class and poorer castes (yes India too) copy them. But there are contingency savings available across all the generations, so debt levels are nowhere near the accepted extremities of American and, to a lesser extent, that of UK private and public debt. In the media, it is thoroughly acceptable to ignore this state of affairs.

If a child "makes it" to a University in China, student debt is not a problem for her. The average Chinese students are paying between $400 and $2,200 per annum in fees to the University, a snip in comparison to £9k here. £27,000+ is a mountainous debt for UK young people who are typically leaving college with these worries and accompanying burden. *Default is the default position* for anyone who goes into low-paid work and that's the majority whilst gig economy rules apply.

We owe this debt hungry position to QE (quantitative easing) and the €uro currency introducing hefty disequilibrium[84] into the global marketplace. Money is far too cheap, owing to the former, and the latter is causing the likes of Italy, Greece, Spain, Ireland, and Portugal to slowly bleed under debt burdens that are too high. Greece, encouragingly, thanks to debt-fuelled tourism, is on the brink of recovery, which in itself is very encouraging news.

Where capital continues to play a crucial role on the one hand, generating profit, the likes of the big 5 (Google, Amazon, Apple, Netflix and Facebook)[85] are not making their equitable contribution, from positions of growing strength, to the tax take[86]. Their accountants spend inordinate amounts of resources and time devising tax avoidance schemes and the global authorities have not classed these as "evasion" and have allowed them over decades to get away with it.

The European Union's Margrithe Vestager has tried to do something about this inherent inequality by slapping huge fines on these companies. Google, for example, has been penalised

---

[84] See bibliography.

[85] As previously "the FAANGS".

[86] Please reference Piketty T, *Capital in the Twenty-first Century* in the bibliography.

for positioning its own ads and vested interests ahead of more honest paying advertisers whose products and services have slipped quietly down the queue. Quite deliberate, exploitative profiteering in 2017 is acceptable and near desirable. By 2019, this status quo is still stable but as Somerset-Webb points out above: reasons to be fearful.

CHAPTER
9

Equity and Flotation Risks: Your other lifeline—how to keep stakeholders happy

Undertaking an Initial Public Offering (IPO) or a more modest flotation on AIM (Alternative Investment Market) in the UK is onerous. You are committing your company to public and media scrutiny and that scrutiny is relentless. The company, if making tidy profit margins, goes from being your smallish, comfortable nest egg to being one big responsibility and potential headache.

You are taking the company into the public domain and, if you're getting large enough, this comes with media and social media scrutiny and critique. For critique (read criticism) it can be a brutal environment to operate in and harsh time horizons (quarterly reporting) can be manic to manage for the bean counters; each individual month-end becomes a race against the clock to make the numbers work. Each quarter-end the share price hangs on a thread again as you race against time to reconcile the numbers.

This is where risk comes in; the sheer pressure of the

deadlines can precipitate wrongdoing under pressure. "Accruals and prepayments" can be adjusted fraudulently and so can inventory. It is best to take a warning on the chin here: under no circumstances be tempted by such easy fixes; this amounts to fraudulent activity[87]. Observe what happened to the "energy giant" Enron in the early noughties. It's chairman, finance director and CEO Jeffrey Skilling were all "at it", creating entities known as special purpose vehicles (SPVs), in order to "park" assets for personal gain and to transmit fraudulent or at least quasi-fraudulent created assets through its balance sheet, enhancing visible profits, boosting share prices and annual bonuses alike. Risk rooted in avarice.

Like any hungry animal feeding a family, growth seems to be all that matters; growing one's income streams to feed the growing family unit. In the West, we seem to have left behind "slow and steady" and it has been undeniably replaced by faster growth and greed *at all costs* in order to achieve the stock market norms of an inflated price/earnings ratio[88]. This is, objectively at any rate, an admirable yet precipitous status quo. Shareholders expect magnificent growth at present and, despite sceptics like me, they are going to price it in up front. Many markets, according to recent research data, are trading at all time or nigh all time high price/earnings ratios, notably the Standard & Poors (S&P) 500.

To elaborate for further context, equity (and bond) markets

---

[87] Though white-collar crime to my mind is not punished sufficiently; some Directors actively treat this situation as an exploitable loophole.

[88] P/e ratio- This is the price of the shares in terms of a multiple of the company's estimated future earnings.

too are essentially run by young men for their own benefit[89]; very few are in it for the long term. Short-term turnover and profit targets are the bane of many a fund manager's life. They disturb long-term positions continuously and their proponents, the stockbrokers, who are also caught up in the greed-trade, also run things for their own benefit rather than for that of the client. This is why the financial services sector is so lucrative; the client or customer is a *third*-class citizen. This is like so in no other industry, all of which try to put the customers at the centre of all activities.

Whilst working at NatWest Securities in the heady 1990s, I used to run and manage the financial and management accounts for a section of the business called "customer liquidity" which had just acquired Fielding, Newson Smith and County Securities to morph into County NatWest, "brokers to the gentry".

At this stage, I was only some five years into my sixteen-year investment banking career. I started then in my sixth year to buy a *Financial Times* and read it every day, to get a grip on both the numbers and the personalities. These two factors were each drivers for the other which makes for a testosterone-filled mania the whole time. This can be hellish wearing on body, mind and spirit. Even when markets were quiet, traders played ruthless, elaborate practical jokes on each other, sat at their desk munching burgers, fries and large full-fat Cokes while many of their companies' brokers, their fund manager clients and their trader friends stood in large, plush champagne bars or pubs drinking, in many cases heavily. Trust me, to serve customer

---

[89] See Bibliography—*Other People's Money* by the *FT*'s John Kay; published 2017.

liquidity was the last priority crossing their minds, except in the literal sense!

Barclays Bank[90] brings out a compendium every year without fail, a large handbook all about equities and UK Treasury Bonds' prices and yields. Tiresome for many, exciting for few.

The Barclays Equity Gilt Study gives a clean picture of returns in both markets over a 116-year period. The data actually goes back a little longer to 1899. "Equities over the longer term have delivered demonstrably better returns than cash or gilts". This is a constant mantra in each volume produced. So you see, equity markets simply cannot be ignored, but it is very disruptive to have young stallions making ruinous prices for clients and avaricious brokers putting funds into the most lucrative instrument for the bank rather than for the client. Thus it was ever so.

Hence, with brokers and bankers spending your cash in bars and restaurants near to where <u>you work,</u> being a (client) fund manager is no picnic. If you miss out versus your stringent benchmarks, i.e. if you do badly or under-perform the markets, you had better have an alternative career lined up; tattered careers litter the square mile. Reference Neil Woodward at the end of June 2019.

---

[90]   *Annual Guide to Equity and Gilt-Edged Markets.* Barclays Bank

CHAPTER 10

Social Media/Hijack Marketing/Fake News: Free of Risks—Never!

Referring to Garry Kasparov's parallels of the game of chess to the challenges presented by the technology-enriched West, I would point the reader at a chunk of chapters which describe Kasparov's battle with Deep Blue, a venture between technology giant IBM and (clearly anonymous) a small clique of chess grand masters (GMs).

One can see the fairy godfather of Gordon Moore stalking the background as Kasparov describes the evolution of the capability of the computer that the Russo-Croatian was up against. In the time period to which I refer, two short years, the machine's complexity moved on considerably as it won the second match having lost the first. The words Artificial Intelligence (AI) have come back into vogue.

The growth of social media mirrors the transformation in intelligence of the Deep Blue machine. As we alluded before, the power of social media has become non-proportionate to "just desserts". This explains the disproportionate airing that fake news (a Trumpism) has been given. Fake news, as experts have reported recently, is nothing new; it has forever been around. What we as the human race have a duty to do is to pay attention and discard the fake stuff since most of the time it is nonsense and obviously bogus.

Hijack or Ambush Marketing

The most prominent example that I have seen in recent years can be plucked from sport. At the time, it became (at City University, London anyway) an all-encompassing case study. It was the ICC World T20 tournament in the West Indies in 2010. I was at the start of what should have been a long journey—a PhD—alas not. I could not deal with the all-consuming need for flowery, ambiguous and pretentious language, but that's another story. One of the reasons that I was required to determine an end to a PhD was my fascination with marketing just after I joined as a freeman of the City of London the Worshipful Company of Marketors. At the time, this gave me unprecedented access to people in the know regarding the London 2012 Olympic Games, its sponsors, its core funders and my other role as business development officer at Ashridge Business School[91] under the Sport Business Initiative header. This was a heady mix of potent positions to straddle and, more importantly, people to chat with and contacts with whom to cement relationships.

West Indies 2010 was a rarity, not least because England won for the first time, and the controversial Kevin Pietersen was man of the series! Returning to my point, the tournament was marked by marketing malpractice; ambush or hijack marketing

---

[91] Now Hult Business School.

was prevalent in and around almost every World Cup venue. The ground sponsors who "owned" the hoardings around the ground for the entire tournament were besieged by competitor brands shamelessly merchandising goods inside the stadia, draped over and obscuring the barriers and perched on top of spectators' heads at give-away prices: free!

In Asia, in particular India, such practices have also taken hold with the ambushers always tending to be young students who are easy prey from consumers' brands at large, high profile events. Betting in sport has assumed a dominant position and Sky own the inflating television rights, inflating the salaries, pumping the risks as well as the gambling addictions.

All the Rage in 2010—The Soccer World Cup (in 2018, in Russia) and Ambush Marketing

An extract from a news story is quoted below:

> "Two Dutch women were released on bail today after facing charges that they organised the ambush marketing stunt that led to 36 orange-clad women being ejected from Soccer City earlier this week.
>
> The women were arrested under the Contravention of Merchandise Marks Act, which prevents companies benefiting from an event without (duly) paying for the advertising. The 36 women were accused of being part of a campaign to promote a Dutch brewery".

The Internet in 2010 was about twenty years of age and had not yet been introduced to TV on demand where, as a consumer, you can now pull down your sport viewing and your film fiestas at any time of the day or night. In those days (only nine years ago), the event was televised on terrestrial TV **and** screened live on satellite (Sky/Fox) TV. It was <u>the event to hijack,</u> especially in the West Indies where ground stewards and police are not at their diligent best.

Having spent some time mulling that infamous Facebook IPO failure in 2012, the crucial factor in many a commercial future is advertisements, readability and stickiness. Advertising success, after all, is how FB has established value-added as a company and maintained a healthy market capitalization.

WPP and its vast array of portfolio agencies are mega-beneficiaries from the online bonanza that is internet and social media advertising. This has transformed advertising business models far faster than many of the incumbents can cope with.

One of the alarm factors in this part of the economy is the "rise" of divisive fake news. As Tim Harford, *The Undercover Economist* extraordinaire, said at the 2017 FTWE festival, *"Fake news I'd agree is old hat, nothing new".*

Share price performances have disregarded the uncertainty around policing imperatives when it comes to internet abuses (FB's market capitalization move . . .) arising from, shall we say, rogue news posts.

Apple? The share price had been stable, then going up quite strongly during late 2016 until the present. The $13bn tax bill levied by the bureaucrats in Brussels, Margrithe Vestager, for tax avoidance it seems, by-passing press journalists, and the company is very busy hiring in London and building in the US.

How to Batten Down the Hatches

This means protection against your immediate risks; in most cases, this translates as your reputation in the marketplace and word of mouth "optimization". Use of loose language online can be lethal. Whatever happens, if you do err, you're going to be quoted out of context. Swearing, off the cuff "jokes" and flippancy are to be discouraged.

Figures and numbers: during interviews formally and informally with journalists, it is advisable to veer away from quoting statistics and financial numbers, the reporting journalists may write, transcribe and print them wrongly. Stranger things have happened and this can be highly embarrassing. Errors are the default when it comes to generalising journalists. They type billions instead of millions and £ instead of $ and these errors often get through their editorial teams with relative ease. By avoiding quoting them or boasting about them, you are nullifying a potential problem.

It is better to speak in plain percentages, such as "an 18% uplift in productivity" or "this translates to 30% more onto the bottom line". Clarity and conciseness works.

CHAPTER 11

Managing and "Exit" Control Long-Term

WHEN IT COMES to this part of the "story" of risk, I hope above all else that you have been engaged and a little entertained even, by my take on the phenomenology of the management and mitigation of risk.

A little anecdote to start us off on the final straight. One abiding memory from my Master's degree year (millennial, 2000) was a www.start-up.com piece regarding an internet "whizz bang". These youngsters (I was a mere 36 at the time) started off a day-long session by openly discussing their "exit strategies" from their businesses. There were two speakers, each from separate companies.

My (naïve) perception at the time was "how arrogant on day 1 to be openly discussing at the safe haven of a leading business school, the exit from one's fledgling commercial venture". Surely this would be "putting the cart before the horse". I'm still dubious to this day about young people who dwell on their speedy exit and their pipe and slippers before they've barely started.

First of all, I could be forgiven for being somewhat old-fashioned when it comes to exiting a business. In a rather staid and stoic way, I would hope (and this hope still lingers) that if I build a business to the point where it is monetizable, I would prepare to pass it down the family through my daughters. Both are capable; one is a budding legal eagle whilst the other is an avid reader and very good at chess. Promising signs.

After the albeit-small initial shock of the above anecdote, you may feel ready to take in some facts about "the exit". As said in the year 1374, reputedly by the one and only Geoffrey Chaucer: *"All good things must come to an end"*. If it is a floundering family business that you have, which through lack of time commitment is allowed to be run into the ground[92], the bank may pull the plug on your working capital one day, so it may be an ignominious business and you go bust, bankrupt or both!

More positively, the business may have hit the best piece of product innovation seen (e.g. the simplistic cat's eye, or the complexity of the iPhone), and you are persuaded by greedy investment advisers to sell part or all of your stake to the stock exchange—go for an initial public offering of shares, an IPO—offering your and/or your partners' stake to stakeholders at large, the general public and investment managers.

In this case, please try:

- to retain some of your stake for your pension plan;
  if the flotation goes astronomically well you shall

---

[92] As the immortal Samuel Butler coined "The way of all flesh" in family businesses in the 1990s to date is to take for granted all the previous generations' hard work and allow the business to wilt whilst milking it for all the cash that you can squeeze out—short termism ad infinitum.

be able to cash in your higher valued chips at a later date.

- to strike a deal (if you do not want to cease working altogether) called an "earn out" whereby you and your expertise are retained in the business for a pre-determined reasonable time on a full or partial salary package and tiered bonus structure, hence the term "earn out".
- not to part with any part of your pension entitlement. Depending on what you chose when you joined/founded your company[93], you'll have a decent final salary (rare), defined benefit or less attractively, defined contribution, or else a meagre stakeholder pension or an equally miserly "workplace pension", which now by law all employers have to offer. It very much depends on how young or mature your company and its schemes are.

Another reasonable path to exit would be to execute a trade sale. Sell the business to a rival or to a start-up or even to a VC (venture capital company) which may want your market share and your lucrative distribution channels at a reasonable price.

Also, in the same vein your business may be subject to a friendly, passive, or even a hostile takeover. Either which way, to see all of these routes as your opportunity to properly crystallise value is your goal; try not to be short-termist and ignorant of future challenges. To reiterate, crystallize as much value as you can; God forbid an asset-stripping venture capitalist (VC).

---

[93] Just remember you were a lot younger at this stage and just maybe you did not pay it an awful lot of attention.

Remember this could still be your best shot at a comfortable lifestyle in retirement, as you pass your peak (it comes to us all). Try to work it out and make it count.

The Danger and the Consequences of the Exit Risks

- Some 84% of assets on a balance sheet (and therefore that are included in the market capitalization of a company) are INTANGIBLE. This is important since losses against this chunk of assets are not insurable and *The Economist* as recently as 25 August 2018 was urging companies to start addressing this. For such an event a new paradigm has to be created; although we can trust the market to undertake this, it will take time. Until then this risk "overhangs" the market, profound but straightforward of fact.

- You may be undervaluing and underselling your stake upon transfer.

- You may be being hassled into the wrong deal long term and miscalculation of personal impact as well as professional.

- You may be selling stock on an Initial Public Offering (of shares) prematurely and at the wrong price (too high as well as too low). Both have damaged businesses in the past.

- You may be signing up to earn-out clauses that undervalue both your legacy and your contribution ongoing, including quite a way into the future.

- *Finally, you may also be completely omitting pension entitlements* from your negotiations and planning.

Mitigation

1. If you can afford to, in-house or externally, take legal advice. Be circumspect of "no-win, no-fee"; many a dead end.
2. Take a tougher stance on your terms and conditions at the outset at all costs; remember, it is important to achieve fair value for your family, colleagues and for yourself.
3. Calculate your own long-term requirements and match them against your liabilities; yes, I'm alluding to pensions and/or your pitifully short endowment policy or even annuity, once more.
4. Due diligence: number one priority for any seller of any thing
    - Credit checks via Experian and for the smaller entities, Dunn & Bradstreet are quite easy to carry out and cheap. They should be in a world in which nearly all inhabitants are overdrawn and in many a case overstretched
    - Informal kicking of tyres: Buy the person a beer and make sure they buy you one back; basic human decency and minimal reciprocity, reinforcing your informal network.
    - Really check them out over those beers. Are their prescient values ones which you respect? Are they cherishing you and above all your staff; your own priorities. Can you really hold up a mirror and say they're definitely taking them into account?
    - Chemistry: is she genuine, do you get and readily give eye contact and is she at ease? Does she really

"get" your ethos and have valid reasons on why she's set aside the funds to buy into it/you?
- I revisit "intangible assets" at this, an appropriate time. How much of her balance sheet is not plant, equipment and the result of profitable sales?

The culture (i.e. the way we get things done around here) is a crucial success factor of any buy out, takeover, merger or even alliance pro tempore. It is so important that this is, for sake of argument, 66%+ a good fit.

Being ruthless about it as entrepreneurs and salesmen alike often are (have historically been and arguably should be), if 33% of people aren't playing ball with your values, get them to check out of your hotel! That includes people inside your tent as well as those outside it.

CHAPTER 12

MiFID 2.0, Basel I, II and III etc.

THE SPHERE OF financial regulation is a mysterious and murky world and there are myriad risks surrounding the various (enormous) documentation(s). Anecdotally, yet in gravity, we used to call the compliance department "the business prevention department". Ironically, at NatWest Securities the Director of this section was called Peter **Blood!**

Origins

The website http://www.cmeregreporting.com is as good a place to begin as any.

Basel I, Basel II AND Basel III all set capital requirements for banks and were introduced in 1988, 2008 and 2010 respectively. This is sometimes 8% and can go up to 10% of banks' monies. It is the government's responsibility to set the capital requirement since it supposedly knows how much risk is effectively "in the system".

The public sector and the private sector get a little muddled here. Basel is a free-world agreement and is monitored by the

BIS, the Bank of International Settlements. They're in charge of systemic risk.

Basel IV—target date of introduction, as yet unknown—This will undoubtedly come in soon (ish). The management of the economy, after all, is the responsibility of the central banks and by their "under-due diligence" they have done us a severe disservice, especially Mark Carney, who seems to think it is in his domain to meddle with politics by managing to orchestrate project fear for Britain exiting the European Union. The risks to the economy of a central banker behaving like this are manifold. The man needs to get a grip and quieten down.

Stress Testing the Banking System

This is a fun game, where the banks stress-test their own system, which somehow doesn't seem quite right to me; this is the sort of self-regulation that we all know does not work. Not least because the bankers simply cannot be trusted to do it thoroughly. It is like England's football team taking penalties in practice; there is simply no one around, no stress for the players concerned and thus the test is pointless; we may as well stop here.

JPMorgan's VaR (value at risk) is the acronym to remember. The maximum loss that a bank can make in one day is determined by the risks it is taking on its proprietary trading positions. Until recently, JPM didn't take monies onto its proprietary books. In this sense, it is a very robust bank; it hedges all its bets effectively and efficiently and its CEO, Jamie Dimon, is seen as something of a hero in banking circles for this very reason. He is a superstar whose wages are **14 times** that of the common man!

Black Swans and Nassim Nicolas Taleb

This author wrote a book in 2008 about trading and "fat tails". He used to be a trader in the financial markets and he knew how to take risks, large ones. What he came to notice was that unexpected events happen in markets all the time. He called them "black swans" as they are supposed to be rare but are, in fact, increasingly common. He talks about dissonance of behaviours, where a trader dares to take a risk then goes into his back office and sets up bogus trading accounts to hide them. This is what the now after-dinner speaker Nick Leeson did at Barings Bank. He lost £900million and bust the bank which was then purchased (glory be) by ING of the Netherlands (who used to be one of my clients). Thea Pronk, take a bow.

He talks about heuristic behaviours where people kid themselves that they are doing OK thus nullifying either their feelings of guilt or their proneness to accidents and fraud.

The author is obstinate in his arrogance; because he took the large risks, he was the one that had to sleep at night, not his compliance people. He did sleep though and in this slumber he conceived a book or two; *Black Swans* was one and *Antifragile* was the other; this is not to mention *The Bed of Procrustes* which was another to be proud of. *Antifragile* is about robustness of attitude, process and strategies/tactics. Taleb describes how people make themselves stronger whilst shaped by deprivation and diversity; they become antifragile.

The Bed of Procrustes tells the story of how human beings tend to "cut risk to size and indeed cut tasks to size", lengthening their bed when it takes longer and cutting off their legs and feet when they're too long (to get into bed with).

Basel IV—The Next Generation of RWA (risk weighted assets)

Finalising Basel III and Evolving Basel IV

This is now an Appendix in order to assist the reader with the "technicals" behind the last two phases of Basel Accords; there will doubtless be more.

This page takes a look at your challenges and our solutions if you're a risk manager or a risk taker in a retail or investment bank. The implementation of the Basel IV framework is already a remarkable challenge for the European banking landscape, as methodologies for the determination of capital requirements are to be revised. In doing so, capital calculations across all risk types will be fundamentally amended.

So, according to many a financial expert and intermediary, the UK is in a "debt crisis", probably the worst since just after the 2007-2008 crisis. The debtors in question "hardly ever ring a credit helpline" until they're sinking or sunk already; that's heuristic human behaviour for you.

One problem being, in the "mixed-race" UK, there is Sharia Law, a Muslim law that does not allow the credit of interest on a bank or any other account. The marketplace has therefore had to devise instruments and accounts that are "Sharia Law compliant". This means that they have only limited capital to spend and it will always come out of the principal element rather than from the interest.

One of UK's pundits, Ms Claer Barrett, recently wrote an article entitled "On the front line with those tackling the UK debt crisis". She ethnographically studied "Pay Plan", a UK credit advisor and she is quite astute here. Debt, her recent piece asserts, is being hidden by nervous husbands from their wives and now (of course) their children; all have vast amounts of debt thanks to their University tuition fees. These (unless

Jeremy Corbyn gets into power) are going up in the foreseeable future rather than falling.

There are of course other advisory bodies, the titles of which often give an insight into the knock-on problems, for example, the *Money and Mental Health Policy Institute*—MMHP for short.

Central Banking—The Future

The banking system will have different central players soon enough with the governmental banks being replaced by MMT, modern monetary theory, where each country will be compelled to manage tax and spend in the cool light of day rather than indulging in "dark arts" like QE (quantitative easing) in order to revive economies. QE by the way is central banker speak for "printing money" and gifting it to the banks to assist with "market liquidity". In 2018, this worked a treat, but in 1929 (the Great Crash) QE was not a perceived option; austerity paralyzed the Western economies and the markets saw shorter working hours and rationing of goods and produce (mainly food and drink). When our ancestors were on the planet, they strove to change things so that future generations could cope but this evolution is slow. Can you imagine today's sixteen-year-olds not being able to buy tea, coffee, bacon and potatoes?

Useful Further Reading

Allen, James. "Figure out your company's make or break strategic problems then use small teams to solve them". *Harvard Business Review* 16 Nov 2017 https://hbr.org/2017/11/figure-out-your-companys-make-or-break-strategic-problems-then-use-small-teams-to-solve-them

Leinwand, Paul and Joachim Rotering. "How to excel at both strategy and execution". *Harvard Business Review* 17 Nov 2017. https://hbr.org/2017/11/how-to-excel-at-both-strategy-and-execution

Leonard, Orla and Layton Wiita. "How the most successful teams bridge the strategy-execution gap". *Harvard Business Review* 23 Nov 2017. https://hbr.org/2017/11/how-the-most-successful-teams-bridge-the-strategy-execution-gap

Mankins, Michael. "Five ways that companies close the strategy/execution gap". *Harvard Business Review* 20 Nov 2017. https://hbr.org/2017/11/5-ways-the-best-companies-close-the-strategy-execution-gap

Martin, Roger L. "CEO's should stop thinking that execution is someone else's job". *Harvard Business Review* 21 Nov 2017. https://hbr.org/2017/11/ceos-should-leave-strategy-to-their-team-and-save-their-focus-for-execution

Great teams thrive on companionship and competence, education and determination, thus say many text books on the subject as well as being well-aired by pundits.

MifID—The Markets in Financial Instruments Directive

I believe that MiFID 1.0 was implemented with the concept of uniting the European Union in terms of the laws and regulations surrounding derivative instruments, plus shares, bonds, units in collective investment schemes and the venue where those instruments are traded.

MiFID applied in the UK from November 2007 and was revised by MiFID II, which took effect in January 2018 to improve the functioning of financial markets in light of the financial crisis and to strengthen investor protection. MiFID

II extended the MiFID requirements in a number of areas including:

- new market structure requirements.
- new and extended requirements in relation to transparency.
- new rules on research and inducements.
- new product governance requirements for manufacturers and distributers of MiFID "products".
- introduction of a harmonised commodity position limits regime.

Britain may live to regret the implementation of this across the EU of which we are trying to get out. The process takes so long though, we may be staying until Halloween on 31st January 2020; that's quite a long time away but will pass quickly. The work behind this from 2007 onwards has been immense by the banks; they are all having to become compliant or close down. Needless to say, most want to stay open.

Merger Risk

At a crucial juncture on the Mifid time-line, Commerzbank and Deutsche Bank announced a merger, but on 2 May 2019 they called a halt. Germans aren't very good at consolidation, besides, one of my former NWS colleagues works at Commerzbank and his job, among thousands of others, would have immediately been under threat.

This is quite a serious point; a lot of the banks' functionality and personnel have been transferred to India. My former colleague has people working for and with him in three different countries!

CHAPTER 13

InfoTech

IN THIS SECTION, we shall look at the crucial role of a country's infotech police. Does the country take cybercrime seriously? The risk to your person or your company of internet-inspired crime—this must be fully mitigated.

Cyber Risks and Hackers

As publication of this document is heralded by continuing authorial anxiety, Russia, formerly the Union of Soviet Socialist Republics, seems to be attempting to revive the Cold War[94].

A caveat from this author's favoured news link, the *Financial Times* [95] on 15 March 2018 read as follows:

> "The FT's Philip Stephens says the Kremlin had nothing to do with the attempted murder of a former Russian

---

[94] The annexation of Crimea occurred on 18 March 2018.

[95] Philip Stephens was the journalist who wrote this rather tongue-in-cheek piece.

spy in the small English city of Salisbury. Moscow must similarly be absolved of any role in the invasion and annexation of Crimea. The heavily-armed Russian soldiers fighting in Eastern Ukraine are no more than civilian volunteers. Cyber attacks in the Baltics and Scandinavia are the invention of hostile states. Russia has no role in the daily slaughter of Syrian civilians. Charges of interference in the US presidential election are wholly fabricated. We know this because Vladimir Putin, the Russian president, insists it to be so."

Moral hazard sometimes does not come into political thinking hence after the "nerve gas poisoning" of a Russian spy and his daughter, **the *Bloomberg* press office** published that a UK cyber-attack upon the Russians was a serious one of three options. Just like many other instances, due to there being no media management in the Mrs May Machine, the *Bloomberg* clerics are dictating controversial potentialities and with Trump in charge, who knows what could happen now. There is here a sense that an existent cold war actually does not exist, in other words, where risk arises, "blame the Russians". The media machine is "in charge of moral hazard" and it is possible that we cannot trust it to get through to the truth.

Cyber-crime is spectacular and it has been überized. Anybody with a fibre optic broadband connection or even an old analogue laptop can launch devastating attacks from almost anywhere.

80% or thereabouts of power, as per the Pareto principle, fall into the hands of 20% of the protagonists. Inequality of "information distribution" spreads across populations in the West, as dark discussions amongst the likes of Cobra Committees take place.

As #BrexitShambles is pushed uphill (vertically) by powerless and inadequate politicians, it is disconcerting, with depleted European alliances that such an attack could be conceived, let alone quickly and successfully executed. This could destabilise the planet just as Donald Trump gets to sit down with Kim Jong-Un, and President Rouhani of Iran, among others.

What is the "Cyber" Threat Exactly?

The Sergei Skripal attack 4 March 2018, in Salisbury UK would be positively Thatcherite in its importance if Mrs May were to pull seamlessly through this spat; remember (and Donald Trump does) <u>Putin is dangerous</u>. Better an ally than a foe he thinks.

Companies—Lipstick on their Collars

A barren landscape on what to do when catastrophe strikes.

The banks (according to a Cyber Security special[96] published in a high quality newspaper[97] just prior to publication of this journal) are busy reading out scripts to customers—in front of others—about the dangers inherent in transferring over £1,500. This is sad and bad for trust levels.

People in banks do not understand why they have to tolerate being spoken to like children and furthermore, the lack of privacy (when there are acres of room all over our high streets) is regrettable. Note my ire and disingenuous sarcasm; this is an outrage.

---

[96] CYBERSECURITY—www.raconteur.net included in *The Sunday Times* 24 February 2019

[97] *The Sunday Times*, May 2019

Computers

Have grown in importance since Moore's law's exponentially steep march. Vast tracts of individual companies' data can be stolen by simply winging it with a small handful of (often) one person's passwords.

Cyber Marketing

Much of this data phishing is, in relative terms, innocent as it relates to (other) companies spam marketing to another's confidential client base. But to learn of key politicians' dinner date preferences and daughters' schools' addresses is quite another matter. Scary.

Financial Payments System Links

As a "fresh" user of the internet back in 1993, I remember the raw feeling of horror when the first "spam scam" arrived. Some reputable source was invoicing me and demanding payment. Now, some twenty-six years later, these techniques have been highly refined by hackers and scammers alike and are landing in my inbox; only some of these are automatically being rerouted to my junk folder.

Of many millions of young, new 2017-2019 internet users, a sizeable minority (without parental interest or attention) are falling straight into the trap. The parents by their absence are literally underwriting the fraud, even though many remain transparently fraudulent.

Western Union Money Transfer outlets are on many a European street; their service transfers money and multi-currency resources across the globe for a fee. It has been noted that monetary fraud and money launderers are a fact of life on its transfer platform also.

International Balance of Payments Statistics

BIS, the Bank of International Settlements, may be another conduit for wrongdoing. As this bank (more a system than an incorporated body) collates collateral and brings standards down to bear upon the international protagonists, individual banks that are incorporated. BIS is fundamental to the "oil" of the international financial landscapes.

Currency Weakness (and Strength)

Many expertise peddlers, including Britain's own Chancellor[98] at the time (2015), predicted a gloomy future for the pound sterling as it leaves the European Union in 2019[99]. The deadline for this "cliff edge" as George Osborne described it is now less than six months away and the £ is trading at 1.2295 vs the US$, still reasonably steady at the lower levels. If the pound were to go back to $1.00, in relatively short order this would really open up trading opportunities with the rest of the world, in particular East Asia and Latin and North America.

Trade should reawaken in short order with North Africa, Britain can probably embrace the rest of the world readily; freed from its European shackles. This would re-invigorate our economy IF it is allowed to happen by the Eurocracy.

---

[98] Mr George Osborne, now Editor in Chief of London's *Evening Standard*—Gamekeeper turned poacher.

[99] Possible but not certain due to occur on 31 October 2019.

Bond Issuance and Money Transfer-Related Fraud (Africa and the Americas)

It is a well-known fact that African states have been neglected and conflicted by the rest of the world over the longer term.

Vanilla theft and Ransom

This is a trifle old fashioned in the land of Artificial Intelligence and *Deep Thinking*. It is still to be reckoned with however; older criminals are sometimes better criminals.

Financial Crime

Now that banks, beyond dispute, are in charge of the global economy, do governments have a role anymore? There is a concise argument to say they do not, (or do I mean should not?) The financial sector does not have the tools to self-regulate, as witness the dilution of first Sarbanes-Oxley and now Dodd Frank and to an extent Basel III[100]. The initiatives that began under Barack Obama after 2008 have now been sprung into reverse by the radical Mr Trump, who desperately wants some evidence to support his persistent campaign promises of economic revival. Sluggish growth does not help his case nor does a reluctance within the Republican echelons to truly give Donald J his head. Would you? By almost three years in, things have altered but only subtly; we have had a "two-year mini boom" but it's all short termism, the (profligate) Central Bankers have warned about putting interest rate rises into

---

[100] *Other People's Money* by John Kay points to the fact however that Financial services creates more legislation habitually in order to make money by guiding users *around* the regulations

reverse. They know there are serious risks if they continue on the incline.

With the loosening of financial regulations and the tax-cutting promises that emerged in 2017, Trump is a liberal; he wants to liberate capital and enterprise to the detriment of everything and everybody else. In the raging 1980s, the same thing happened[101], but things have moved on and underneath all the hype, everything is fragile, everything. Most families in UK, Europe and the US are just one or two months' salary deprivation away from financial ruin. This is being preluded by a period of hardship for consumer borrowers who are beginning to feel the pinch of the first throes of fiscal tightening.

At such times, crime hits hard. Software is being installed to cash machines to retain and regurgitate people's PIN numbers, people completing large real estate transactions are having their completion monies stolen through the disbursement of bogus but authentic-looking emails. Pensions are being stolen just prior to beneficiary withdrawals, leaving pensioners who have toiled indefatigably to fend for themselves with little or no money (or expanding debts). Contactless debit cards and software are not helping us, nor too is people's over-dependence on their mobile phones. I would by way of illustration never tie myself to Paypal nor Applepay, both of these providers are besieged with copycat and original criminal scams; the system has been prised open for abuse.

The regulators, giving credit where credit is due, were prompt to act after the 2007-2008 financial meltdown; these bodies quickly instituted "The Emergency Economic Stabilization Act of 2008", and further extended the Sarbanes Oxley act which

---

[101] Cf President Ronald Reagan

"experts" are now saying is affecting US competitiveness in the capital markets. The very phraseology used in the Fundamental Principles of Financial Regulation [102]indicates the controlling influence of the investment banks.

Machine Growth—Intelligence Wise

Although not fully developed through (chess guru) Garry Kasparov's book, the theme of growth in the artificial intelligence sphere is a thread that runs through *Deep Thinking*. One of the key differentiators of machine from human intelligence is the decrease in concentration in the human as fatigue kicks in. Computers on the other hand are indefatigable. Reliability is thus superior on the computerized side of things.

"A growing number of rechargeable batteries in time need to be recycled".

The reputation of ALL car makers will get tied into this risk, i.e. the marketing strut and arrogance of the vanilla car manufacturers are to be hooked into the fact that they will not invest sufficiently in battery and the inherently necessary recharge and recycling technologies. Tesla Inc. in August 2018, announced to the world via Elon Musk's (Founder) tweet, that it was to take the company private again—"funding secured". As ever with certain entrepreneurs, Musk was dreaming/

---

[102] Authored by: Markus Brunnermeier, Princeton University Andrew Crocket, JPMorgan Chase Charles Goodhart, London School of Economics Martin Hellwig, Max Planck Institute Avinash D. Persaud, Chairman. Intelligence Capital Limited Hyun Shin, Princeton University: *The Geneva Report on the World Economy 11*.

deluded and exaggerating. The company after burning through hundreds of $millions in cash, finally begun to hit its long-elusive production targets. The market in the stock rocketed up with the privatisation news, volatility was introduced, the equity continued to gyrate.

Perilous

Now we do not have to acquire the skills and connivance of a hacker to procure serious assets. Contactless debit cards can be widely acquired on the streets (that's theft though) but one can purchase several items under £30 within a few hours of the find and get away with it. With incomes dwindling and job opportunities so scarce it is petty crime that some are turning to in these straightened times. Beware. The police forces are so under-resourced that petty crime prevention is shifting to "online only".

The Facebook privacy crisis broke 23 March 2018. Watcheth this space. In high streets up and down, the UK can be seen the advertisement "Facebook: Fake News is Not Our Friend". A fleeting sign of the company's budget strength that they can flood UK high streets with subtle advertising just like that.

Added to this looseness is voice recognition technology. According to an *Economist* study[103] it only takes 7 seconds of voice footage to be able to impersonate someone else long enough to break through typical VOIP technology security. This is alarming and I cannot see readily any mitigating methods, apart from checking bank balances daily and not

---

[103] *I Hear You—Speech Recognition*—The Economist Journal 5 January 2017

taking up the offer of recording your voice as your account's security mechanism.

Approach

The objective when this book was begun and still now is to discuss clear and present danger in an engaging and exciting way. If you're unhappy thus far please tweet your displeasure and / or suggestions to @peachyrob.

CHAPTER 14

Governance and Related Risks

IN THE PRIVATE sector—which after all pays for the government—things never had a propensity to self-regulate. Nowadays there is little trust left with them. On the exact same day as Marks and Spencer's plc left the FTSE100 Index, I find this fact disturbing.

As you will already have gathered from my tone, not too many politicians after the expenses scandal could be adequately trusted to regulate the government itself and a still cumbersome public sector.

As you will also have gathered from your reading to date, the charities sector's governance is woeful, some might say shambolic. Billions are raised worldwide for international development charities, of which I used to work for two: The British Executive Service Overseas and then Voluntary Service Overseas as the former was swallowed by the latter. BESO and VSO though were increasingly DfID funded—in the former case 70% and in the latter, probably 65%.

As far as governance is concerned, both were pretty good and had firm chairs of trustees. When the charity was seeking less public sector support and dependency, I introduced (with the help of my Marketing Director) The John Ellerman Foundation. This was an exemplary piece of work because (rare at the time) the foundation funded "core costs". We approached them firmly on the front foot: Would they be interested in funding the *merger costs* of the two organisations? Please?

The answer came back from Chairman Tim Glass, a firm "yes". The bid took seventeen draftings to prepare across the two organisations and many a trip to VSO's HQ in Putney. As we were preparing information for the bid, I pleaded for governance transparency; we would have to merge the two boards of trustees which would entail the loss of a few, albeit voluntary Trustees. Added to this there would have to be significant redundancies among the staff and consultants (of which I was one). Once again a fact of life; oh dear, how sad, never mind!

We received (on my last day) a pristine cheque for £100,000; magnificent though this was, I had to move on. Still, on the same day, I received a call from a chap called Michael Rawlinson of Charity Fundraising Appointment (CFA); intriguingly, they were based in Gracechurch Street in the City. The CEO at the time was Mr Richard Evans, now a good friend. Both Michael and Richard wanted me to go for a new role as Trust Director (responsible for all fundraising and day-to-day operations) for the Challenger Trust, a UK Registered charity (#1068226) for whom I did some work in July and early August 2019, that's fourteen years on from when I started; a sound *informal* network.

Needless to say, in a chapter on governance: I was conflicted. My salary was being fully met by a private company (World Challenge Expeditions Ltd) yet my responsibility was to Mr Felix Francis (son of famous author Dick). Interesting.

As Charles Handy taught me (through reading his masterful books) being conflicted at work in a dual role is a nightmare. First there are the practicalities: how long should I stay domiciled in WCE's offices? Should I talk to the staff and consultants there? The culture in the company was energetic, Rawlinson had told me, and the place was always abuzz with activity, but little old me was rather anxious about my situation.

I decided to air my concerns to the company's CEO, Charles Rigby. Now, he seemed rather relaxed about the whole thing. Felix was too.

Then, after a mere four weeks at the World Challenge Offices, I was asked by Charles, "Where is first £5,000 I was nonplussed. Surely he, the founder of World Challenge Expeditions would understand that fundraising is about people and a four-week time horizon is but a tick in time.

Fifteen weeks later, my first £5,000 arrived from the Mercers' Livery Company; again in the City of London. Result!

Around Easter time (that's four months in), my next £12,000 arrived from, again, the private sector company BHP Billiton plc. Broken Hill Propriety of Australia had merged with Billiton Ltd to become one company. Another complexity to deal with. No problem though. The CSR Director in London answered her own telephone, so I went straight into my elevator pitch. My risk here was delivering a pitch without a trustee or a manager present. My maturity (I was 41 at the time) counted in my favour as did my silver hair!

On 5 July 2005—that's 15 months later—my third cheque arrived (electronically by now) in the amount of US$200,000.00. There was $400,000 to come in 2007!

Suffice it to say, yours truly was up on cloud 9 by now.

I then, as was my wont, went on a three-and-a-half week vacation to New Zealand to watch the British & Irish Lions take on the mighty New Zealand All-Blacks.

The Crux—My Governance Issues

The CFO of World Challenge was promoted to COO of World Challenge and he certainly wasn't going to make life easier for me, even though he sanctioned me a pay rise, in line with all the other employees, of course. What really got Nigel's goat was my monthly expense claims. I wasn't on the fiddle(!) but I had got into the (healthy) habit of posting my receipts in and attaching them with totals to Challenger Trust-headed notepaper. Miller was no governance expert but I believe he should have known better than to quibble and get wound up about such a trifling matter.

In my day-to-day role, much of my work took place remotely (in London, based at the Institute of Directors, where I was a member) and attending meetings with potential donors constantly. One, in fact, was just across the road: Reed Elsevier plc at No. 3 the Strand.

By the time mid-2005 came around, Felix Francis had been binned off by World Challenge and was also (forcibly and aggressively) stood down as Trustee Chairman. He was replaced by a WCE CEO-ally, and all of this took place behind my back whilst I was away.

I was then told that there was a three-line whip in place for a corporate away day (three actually) down in Southampton aboard a moored ship there. Rather sensibly, in my opinion, I wanted to keep this at arm's length. The company was sponsoring my salary that was all; it was not supposed remotely, to be courting me or "converting" me to their company culture yet that was what Miller, the CEO and Hayward,[104] were doing.

---

[104] https://www.linkedin.com/in/terryhayward/

Sensibly again, following up on a very warm lead from an associate, I had booked a meeting in Harrow with the headmaster at the John Lyon's School. I dutifully drove back to Berkhamsted after supper and scooted off for the meeting next morning in my car.

I was then reprimanded for leaving the away days prematurely even though my chairman had agreed to this. The company was loaning to me a pleasant young lady to help me on bids, research and administration; this resource was cut back to about a half-day a week... Insufficient.

WCE wanted to pay me a bonus in 2005. I turned this opportunity down since I was, I said, not in the business of making excess money in the name of charity. My sales director (Hayward) was raging and told the Chief Executive so.

Very shortly after this, I was called by CEO Charlie Rigby on my day off (a recharge-the-batteries day shopping and smooching with my wife) and looking forward to a productive lead up to Christmas. I was to be proved wrong.

There had been talk all year of hosting a Challenger Trust fundraising lunch/ dinner; no expense spared. But this did not compute to me! Rigby rang me very early one morning whilst I was on a donor visit and told me that under no circumstances was I to invite Felix Francis to the dinner. I duly rang and left a message and also emailed Francis.

Charlie ordered me to stop the car and discuss this with him. He then launched into raging invective criticising my diplomatic skills and was generally "on my case". I was thus distraught and yes, still conflicted day to day.

Jerry Witcher, a World Challenge sales manager and I needed to talk, so I drove over to Hitchin in Hertfordshire to see him and have a sandwich/coffees. Jerry then went on to confide in me about bullying from Rigby (before my time at

Challenger). It transpired—why could I not see it at the time?—that Charlie was:

1. Going to try to sell World Challenge profitably and yes again, ruthlessly[105].
2. Intended to treat the Challenger Trust as his baby as well as his "retirement project".

Thenceforth the wheels came off. I continued to receive many donations, even from friends who had been at and partook in my version of a charity lunch:

- Great food.
- People who like and respect me and the work that I was doing at the trust.
- Beneficiaries—about five young people aged 9-19 who benefitted from the Trust's bursaries.
- The board of Challenger Trust.
- Wealthy and poorer friends of mine.
- Great wine.
- Relationship-building with many potential donors.
- A superb after-lunch speaker: Horace Woody-Brock, a non-exec at Goldman Sachs. All good.

There has been a favourable end to the World Challenge Expeditions story. Charles Rigby, post the sale of WCE has founded and funded a new company Contour Educational Services and continues as Chairman of the Challenger Trust,

---

[105] World Challenge was sold to Tui Travel in 2006 for a premier price.

which I very effectively helped him re-launch in 2004. I am attending his newest relaunch of *"Mayflower400"* where Mr Rigby is planning to take 2 quite large cohorts of "transition sensitive" 16 to 18 year-olds on 2 x 48 day voyages from Plymouth UK to Plymouth USA. This has been carefully thought through and it is not inconceivable that I can assist again with the successful progress of the Challenger Trust, UK Charity Number 1068226—please look them up, these are very exciting proposals being recommended. All is forgiven Charlie, all's well that ends well and no hard feelings.

Private Companies' Governance

This is a different kettle of fish when it comes to due diligence and professionalism. The first thing to say is that broadly, private companies have boards that are on the large side; meetings drag out for hours and importantly, decisions, crucial decisions are taken when many of the deciders are dog-tired.

The secret to swift and efficient action here is to use sub-committees. These are small groups (twos and threes) and they laser in on necessary agendas and generally can work a lot faster.

There are several, long-standing, other problems at board level in privately owned companies:

- The CEO and the Founder are one and the same person.
- None of the subordinate board personnel stand up to him/her.
- Decisions are taken outside of the convening forum (a fait accompli).

- Absentees are not brought up to speed.
- Minutes of board meetings are often inaccurate and therefore go UN-actioned.

This is when it is all about the chair's leadership qualities. Often, when people are ignored, they have quality input; equally those that are the loudest are often spraying hot air around the forum.

Effectiveness is a forgotten quality, the organisation as a whole can lose focus and therefore miss objectives.

Public Sector Governance—Government?

Now, as they say in the UK, and US, here is a different ball game altogether. Taking one back to 2003 or thereabouts there were two sides to the coin: government and citizens. By 2019, there are a multitude of stakeholders that complicate the situation.

There are NGOs, i.e. organisations that are not part of the government and campaign against (often) the government of the day. There are third sector social enterprises[106] whose governance is often 50% private enterprise, 25% government funded and 25% charity focused; it's a melee!

Then, confusingly some might say, there are QUANGO's, an invention of Labour Administrations; these are quasi-non-governmental organisations. Their governance is often a) narrowly held and b) lacking in any real "teeth" or traction.

---

[106] I did year 1 of a PhD at the University of Durham in this subject but due to the liquidation and receivership of my research company I was not able to finish it.

Corporate Governance—A potted history

Company Law

Introduction

The Financial Reporting Council has recently promulgated its revised UK Corporate Governance Code (by way of amendment of the Combined Code). The Code is the primary set of corporate governance principles applicable to listed companies with a premium listing on the London Stock Exchange notwithstanding the place where the company is incorporated.

Corporate Governance

Governance is a word that scarcely existed 30 years ago. Corporate governance is commonly regarded as "the entire framework within which companies operate" [1].

It is also considered as "concerned with holding the balance between economic and social aims. The governance framework is there to promote the effective use of resources and equally to require responsibility and the stewardship of those resources. The goal is to align as nearly as possible the benefits of individuals, corporations and society" [2].

However, the UK Corporate Governance Code, being one of the most important instruments regulating this field of law, is still not a kind of legislation. And its predecessor, the Combined Code has never been. It was not passed by the Parliament either but came from the committees representing business and financial interests and it is invoked only to the companies, listed above, and only within the boundaries of the principle of "comply or explain".

Historical Review

Nevertheless, history of the Code and Scandals that led to its introduction were rather celebrated.

The "overturn" began in the early 1990s with the innovative report from Sir Adrian Cadbury considering the financial aspects of the corporate governance. Aimed at listed companies and accounting especially on standards of corporate conduct and ethics, the "Cadbury Code" was gradually accepted by the City and the Stock Exchange and, in 1998, after further reports, it developed into the Combined Code on Corporate Governance.

The Cadbury Committee [3] consisted of the London Stock Exchange, the Financial Reporting Council and the accountancy profession. This Commission appeared mostly as a result of the Maxwell scandal [4], where the director, Mr. Maxwell, had been found unsuited for the position of a director. Regrettably, but in 1971 this characteristic was actually assigned to him, and there was no legislative act that could have dismissed him from the position of a director. Consequently, 550 million pounds went missing due to inappropriate management. Maxwell was "lost at sea," but many believe that he took his own life as a result of this.

In the Greenbury Report and the Hampel Report, the issue of remuneration was raised and a revision of the previous recommendations of the Committees took place, resulting in having principles of good governance rather than explicit regulations. The Combined Code of 1998 encompassed the principles and recommendations of the Cadbury, Greenbury and Hampel reports altogether.

Thus, by 2003, sections had been added on payments, risk control, internal management and audit committees.

Almost simultaneously, the Company Act was passed and

has now become a law. This act permits companies more flexibility in choosing the ways they operate. For example, written directives signed by the shareholders are an alternative to calling general meetings and is regarded as making it much simpler to use them. Written directives will no longer need to be approved by each of the shareholders. Besides, companies can use electronic methods of record-keeping. Directives and resolutions may be circulated by email or by websites, but with the shareholder's consent. This amendment is undoubtedly speeding up the decision making process overall.

Walker Report

In 2008, the banking crisis and the efficient nationalisation of some UK banks caused the government to ask Sir David Walker to look in separately at corporate governance in UK banks and other significant financial institutions [5] . That caused more fundamental revision of the Code by the Financial Reporting Council. A new wording duly came out, this time with a new title: **the UK Corporate Governance Code.**

More concretely, Walker strove to look at:

- how to *perfect r*isk control at the board level;
- whether incentive and bonus programmes *promote risk* undertaking;
- the proper balance of abilities, experience and independence on a board of directors;
- the position of institutional shareholders in relation with and monitoring boards of directors.

All in all, the 2009 Walker Report created 39 useful recommendations for better corporate governance. It's important to point out that they were mostly aimed at banks, huge insurance institutions and other financial establishments. Some of them were commonly appropriate for companies of other sectors and therefore feature in the FRC's UK Corporate Governance Code of June 2010; others will operate as simple examples of best practice in particular cases.

That was another attempt to improve the already existing system of control over the benefits of the participants involved in a company and it is an integration of all the previous attempts. It dealt with different aspects of the board structure, the internal management and a number of the best feasible manners to perfect corporate governance for listed PLCs.

In accordance with the Code, the positions of the chairman and the managing director were to be held by ***different individuals***[107], with clearly different roles between them so that there can be a better control over their deeds. Of course these two positions could be held by the same person but the grounds on this had to be explained, because it was evidently much easier to abuse the power when these two important positions were held by the same individual, as in the event of Polly Peck, where Asil Nadir had all the power in his hands. The result of this was the fact that no one could control him and he easily abused it, creating the so-called "Polly Peck scandal" [6].

In this scandal, the product of the electronics multinational company established by Nadir, collapsed with £1 billion of

---

[107] There are many companies which blithely ignore the code here; this is not ideal but the government has been increasingly reluctant to interfere here. Sports Direct is a salient example which doesn't run well and whose chair and CEO is also the owner of Newcastle Football Club—Imagine all the free advertising! Mike Ashley doesn't have to.

formerly undeclared debts. Asil Nadir, the Chief Director of the company, was accused of theft amounting to £34 million. These scandals encouraged the Cadbury Committee to introduce at least three non-executive directors' positions and to fix that the positions of Chairman of the Board and Chief Executive Officer of these companies are to be held by two different persons [7].

In the Code, the issue of remuneration was also touched upon. Under this document, there had to be a transparent and formal course for the remuneration of the directors and there had to be a remuneration committee composed of non-executive directors as well that will set up the remuneration level for each individual director separately. Moreover, this remuneration course had to be included into the annual report on the company. The issue of remuneration is known to have been set up in the Code as a result of the next "scandal" in the field of corporate governance, called "Tyco Scandal" [8]. Reportedly, once the Chairman of the company appeared to be involved in using the company's assets to *buy homes and rare artworks for the executives*. Mr. Kozlowski, the chief director of the company has habitually abused his position and caused Tyco to expend lots of money for his personal benefit.

The Issue of Non-executives

The use of non- executive directors was merely one of possible manners of perfecting the internal administration by providing new ideas and giving more efficient proposals, making sure that the suitable procedures are kept and that the executives are appropriately trained, as they will have independent board members who will criticise their actions and attempts and skills for running the company successfully. The board had to have at least two non-executives[108] if it isn't a big company and up to half the board of directors for the large companies. Those amendments were rather appropriate, since in the Wyevale Company an unsuitable director and two non-executive directors were actually dismissed by the non-executive directors.

It should be noted that NEDs are directors without additional administrative positions in the company. They were first considered as a solution to the corporate management problems and to the continuous scandals of the "Cadbury Committee" and they still are one of the most famous solutions of the Code. These NEDs are remunerated lavishly, some may say—A minimum of £12,000—£25,000 for just twelve days work a year; nice work if you can get it!

The NEDs surely should be independent, but there is and always will be a big question whether they can be independent altogether. The non-executives are usually appointed by the executives and the shareholders from the range of non-executive directors being recommended by other fellow executive directors; they are commonly of the same educational, social and business environment as the executives, and moreover, they once have been the executive directors previously by themselves. That will evidently make it burdensome for them to check the decisions of the executives and cancel/amend them, as they already have an amicable relationship with the executives. Moreover, the non-executives are dependent on the information that they are supplied with by the executives. Even if they want to check up the information in detail as the non-executives—this happens in many companies, and are able to examine the affairs of a company—they'll need lots

---

[108] Known as NEDs now

of time and persistence to check the actions of the company every day. That factually makes them inefficient, being inappropriate and deprived of the necessary information and the time to deal with each company; therefore, they are commonly unable to have an adequate control over the company's affairs.

There is another matter that is the responsibility of the NEDs. The thing is, under the Code, their responsibility sharply differs from their workload, the time and the information they usually have access to. That makes the non-executives more lenient towards their duties, taking into account the amount of remuneration they get, because it's obvious that their payment is not at the same level with that of the executives. Besides, they have relatively little responsibility towards the shareholders. They are PAID to be and demonstrate objectivity, criticise and blame. Whistle-blowers have been more a feature of late; an NED is an onerous responsibility.

It appears that the code has a broadly beneficial impact regarding the companies and investors. It acknowledged better standards of governance generally, and the "comply or explain" approach is working actually well, as the activity of the companies can be evaluated by the quality level of the explanations they give. Moreover, it is obligatory to proceed to control over the accuracy of the "comply or explain" practice, which appears to be of great significance. Besides, there is undoubtedly positive change in the quality of disclosure by the companies, even if there is still a large place for improvement as is stated by investors and observers. All in all, the Code has been very successfully introduced.

Notwithstanding the fact that the Code was frequently argued to be too detailed and insufficiently flexible for being effective in corporate governance, this seems to be irrelevant for these companies now. On the other hand, even if the Code is too detailed, it still does not cover several significant parts that interest investors. In fact, the Code *not* being a kind of legislation and being not legally binding, cannot be so easily enforced if the company does not want to comply with it.

The UK Corporate Governance Code of 2010

Not being fundamentally re-written, the UK Corporate Governance Code of 2010, however, has undergone several significant changes. Among them:

a. new principles, for example, the position of non-executive directors in challenging and developing the strategy;
b. amendments to existing principles, for example, boards must take into consideration the benefits of gender and other distinctions while making appointments;
c. amendments to Code provisions, the most notable of which is surely a new proposal of yearly re-election of all directors;
d. each company with a Premium Listing on the London Stock Exchange should either "comply" or "explain" with the new Code as regards the financial years beginning after June 2010.

However, it's probably worth noting that a new section considering this principle in comparison with the previous reading of the Code. Thus, a new Code recognizes that "non-compliance" can be justified in case if proper corporate governance may be reached in other manners. Herewith, the company must "clearly and carefully" explain the grounds for such non-compliance to shareholders and must aim to represent how its practice is consistent with the corresponding principle and promote right management. Simultaneously, it has to be mentioned that the Code accommodates also a rather sensible response to the financial crisis, namely, it has increased emphasis on the position of the chairman, the necessity of constructive challenge from non-executive directors, and the central position of the board in risk control. However, the Code incorporated also some provisions, of which the scientists were not very pleased.[109]

First of all, it goes about a new requirement for the yearly election of the entire board. Under the former legislation, the most directors were actually re-elected only every third year. This very provision is supposed to intensify a short-termist mentality amongst directors, and contradicts the other Code principles (and company law) promoting the board to concentrate on "the long-term success of the company."

Now a new Code has different point considering the remuneration. Thus, the performance-related parts of the executives' remuneration are to be formed in such a way to promote the long-term development, and being stretching. At the same time, the Code of 2010 discourages all possible forms of performance-related payments for the non-executive directors, not only the options [9]. In addition, now the

---

[109] All this somewhat wishy washy language covers up the fact that the Code is susceptible to considerable abuse, as recent episodes in the US and UK have demonstrated. Since 2008 much of the 2010 regulation that took place has either been relaxed or withdrawn, to clarify, the banks drive this relaxation not the companies themselves.

chairman has to ensure that all directors are aware of their shareholders' problems and interests, while previously, the chairman and other "directors as appropriate" were demanded just to maintain contact with the shareholders.

Conclusions

To conclude, the revised Code has finally been improved significantly but still there are some uncovered issues that are to be regulated and existing problems in the sphere of corporate governance to solve. Even if it is not legally binding, it still is followed by most of the companies and with the help of the London Stock Exchange, it is not easy to break the principles set up in the UK Corporate Governance Code. That surely means that the Code is rather effective in practice nowadays. Of course, the "comply or explain" rule provides the opportunity for companies to evade the Code; however, they are judged by investors and official bodies taking into account their explanations. And if the explanations are not precise enough, the company won't be able attract investors and would be under permanent control of the London Stock Exchange and all the other state bodies involved in business.

This precis has come courtesy of Lawteacher.net[110] to whom I would like to convey my thanks.

I hope that the reader can see how "hole-ridden" legislation is here. Directors appoint NEDs who are the same as them; often white Anglo-Saxon males in whose company they feel comfortable. It is up to these people in 2019

---

[110] https://www.lawteacher.net/free-law-essays/company-law/do-the-uk-corporate-governance-law-essays.php

and beyond to control, criticise and blow the whistle when needed.

FT Stop Press: In an interview with the *Weekend FT*'s journalist, one CEO (of a Dutch company) stated that the secret of being able to go from good to great is "GOOD GOVERNANCE AND EXCELLENT EXECUTION".

SUMMARY

It is to be hoped that this manual or "Handbook" serves as a relatively quick and succinct guide to risks in the global markets and economies as they relate to all of us. Many more of these than previously are migrating into digital communications and people are nervous. The terror alert is forever pointing at "CRITICAL" or "SEVERE" and people are in turn desperate and vulnerable.

Please be advised that I am very grateful that you made it to the end of my little Handbook.

Happy Hunting and as ever, please Be Very Careful!

APPENDIX

Brexit

Markets don't like uncertainty and the way the banks have been bleating about having to de-camp some operations to mainland Europe you can tell the not-so-poor buggers are upset. Diddums!

The threat of fin-tech over the entire status quo of fund management and bankers' business models is clear but obviously being played down by the media and PR people: vested interests. *City A.M.*, *The Economist* and the *Financial Times* are all three definitely Remoaners, though the former talks of promising ASEAN alliances and of London's enduring qualities as a long-term financial capital and hub of the world, sentiments with which I would agree.

Case studies

Policies and People

1980-2018—yes, including this year, 2019, it is arguable that "all the world's a Ponzi scheme". Or at least it is in the West. President Ronald Reagan and Mrs Margaret Thatcher's market-led revolution in Western economies was, as my friend Horace Woody Brock says, a bad idea that led to bad policies. The

Western democracies and especially those trapped by heavy bureaucracy *the EU* are stagnant, not fully so but headed that way.

H (Woody) Brock's book *American Gridlock*—whose cover design is genius—was largely under-covered and ignored.

Woody is a bit of a market "bear" and is acutely conscious in his writing of America's fixation on debt levels—they are at peaks—so is the budget deficit. He bemoans—though not in this book [111]—the necessity of all young people to take a lavish gap year as an alternative to earning and taking lavish holidays abroad where a stay-cation would do. His focus and his stare are scary; he is a very clever man who has advised senior level governments on both sides of the Atlantic.

3G and 4G Sales of National Licenses to Telecoms Companies

Mobile-friendly 4G connectivity to users across the UK. Ofcom is the telecommunications regulator in the UK and it is responsible for the coordination of the auction. There were five winning bidders.

After more than fifty rounds of bidding, EE, Everything Everywhere Ltd, Hutchison 3G UK Ltd, Niche Spectrum Ventures Ltd (a subsidiary of BT Group plc), Telefónica UK Ltd and Vodafone Ltd have all won spectrum. This is suitable for rolling out new superfast mobile broadband services to consumers and to small and large businesses across the UK1.

---

[111] This was quoted at an "after-lunch" speech that Mr Woody-Brock made for the Challenger Trust an outdoor experiential learning charity of which I was Trust Director.

Due to the mobile capacity and improved speeds this was long and eagerly awaited by the bidders.
The 250mhz was sold for £2.341bn

EE	£588.90Million
Hutchison 3	£225Million
BT	£186.47Million
Telefonica	£550Million
Vodafone	£790.76Million

Risks in Bidding

The inherent risks in making a bid for the network capacity is not matching the numbers of customers onto the "grid" in the numbers of capacity—i.e. a shortage of buyers when as a provider, you need to fill all of your purchased MhZs.

Ofcom as the government body was the recipient of the £2.341.13bn in February 2013.

Over the coming six years, some £20bn of value will have been realised (by 2023). Evidently the bid price looks around fair value. The speed and efficiency of 3G and 4G networks will be researched over the years in order to ensure that customers are receiving optimum service speeds. We are told that 5G changes everything.

The relevant legislation behind the broadband sales can be found in the government's Wireless Telegraphy Act 2006 (Directions to Ofcom) Order 2010.

It has probably been forgotten but back in the 1990s Vodafone plc purchased Mannesman of Germany in one of not-too-many cross-border mega-mergers. This is one of the reasons why VODS was the kingpin bidder.

Four years after the bidding was settled, the Vodafone

reach has expanded appropriately and the marketing arm is probably the most aggressive of the 5 holders of licences. Its pricing is very keen but then in marketing terms EE and O2 were in the pole positions at the time of the settlement in 2013.

Facebook's Disastrous IPO

Now worth well in advance of $226bn on the American stock markets, the Mark Zuckerberg-founded company has clearly come through the dark woods and out the other side. Reid Hoffman, a founding investor, described the early life episode as a rather "egregious fuck up". The opening stock price of $38 seemed rich for the various investment bankers who had "missed the business". Morgan Stanley, four years after the financial crisis came to a head, was suspected of artificially scaffolding the price. Peter Thiel, the founder of PayPal, cashed in his Facebook chips on day one at $500m, *a thousand times* the half-million dollars that he had invested. In many ways, the tale of the stock price's demise was more than a little farcical. There was, coincidence had it, a "technical glitch" on the opening bell which delayed the start of trading by 45 minutes.

There were mixed expectations on the stock price trading. Many expected a return to the 1980s where "stagging" was commonplace. That is placing the stock at an artificial premium, selling the key stakes at the higher levels before a same-day plummeting which brings investors sharply down to earth. This is a widespread and disruptive practice and holds no respect for an honest longer-term investor. It also unnerves the short-termers. The opening days of trading can be anxious times.

Others speculated upon a "pop" where the stock immediately

zings up to another level; a basis change as a trader would have it. Stock loaned against collateral, which technically allows the fund manager to sell the stock without buying it, must have been of a frenzy, as one boasted of selling equities just after the belated opening bell at $42.00. Hedge funds that shorted explained that Google's p/earnings ratio was 6 times profits, whereas Facebook's, which was supposedly twice as profitable, was trading at 24x earnings. Speculators moved swiftly in on the open and shorted the securities; waiting patiently if necessary to buy them back cheaper later.

The bankers, as they did in 2008, had messed up; yes, they had been propping up the share price to the higher level, drafting bull market reports on future performance and indulging in over-hype. The earnings downgrades which the bankers had discovered had, for purely avaricious reasons been hushed up, the market was not to know while buyers were in the throes of being warmed up—nicely! Lawsuits by investors went up from just five in the early days after to forty in exceptionally short order. Some of this was unprecedented; people in the backrooms must have been shivering with fear.

Underneath the concern, they had unearthed major strategy confusion at Facebook. Founder Zuckerberg used to discuss ceaselessly with his peers what business they were in (?). Surely when you are just about to place millions of shares with an excitable public, you would have lucid answers to these questions; not Zuckerberg.

Today we sit seven years on and wiser. The company has decided that it is the largest social network the world has ever seen and by several clever purchases it has tied in most of its potential competitors to its own business. Hence, technically the website really does its job; it is no longer clunky and works like a dream on a smart phone, must haves for every teenager from thirteen up to 55 years old!

Elon Musk, 2018—A Turning Point for the Serial Entrepreneur

The Tesla Motor Company is arguably in trouble. In the middle of the week on a quiet stock market day, Mr Musk took hold of his smart phone and tweeted words to the effect of: *"I am thinking about taking Tesla private again, funding secured."* The trouble was, and still is, that at current prices and p/e ratios, this means raising $82billion. Bankers are hardly going to "roll" this over to him.

He is now being accused of creating opportunistic "fake news", that may pump the price up. Stock price volatility would have doubtless gone up since:

The implied volatility of the stock options is a shocking 57.9% on today's stock level and volumes. Trading volumes are spiking as speculators galore get involved. They will have to be careful; there will be some big moves. Tesla's risk exposure is all about one thing—liquidity. The company has little cash and no doubt has "offsets" which depend on Musk's SpaceEx's cash generation, which, given he wants to take a rocket to Mars, is very sparse. The company is indebted indeed and equally has very little cash.

So the "vol"[112] in the index options' implied volatility tells a tale in itself; the market and its traders crave certainty and where there is little, call option and put option prices spike as a result.

There has scarcely been as much coverage of a single stock/CEO in the quality press; all the quality journalists are second guessing where next for Tesla and Musk. One advocated stepping Musk back from the business and putting in an

---

[112] Volatility—'tending to fluctuate sharply and regularly

"acting" CEO. It is all a question of the board standing up to the founder. Many a company has struggled with this challenge but it takes a strong chairman and a supportive executive to pull off alterations such as this.

Goldman Sachs, August 1998

Goldman Sachs' botched IPO of 1998. Coming as it *didn't*, ten years before the subprime lending crisis, this attempted placing wasn't the end of Goldman's attempts to go semi-public. The bank eventually succeeded in the endeavour a year later when the worst "shocks" were over. John Corzine and Hank Paulson, two heavyweight investment bankers, were at the helm at the time, so it really should not have gone away. The $70bn mega-merger of Citigroup and Travellers had just gone through straight, back in the heady days of the late 1990s. At the time, Goldman Sachs had 129 years of private banking history. It turns out that it didn't relinquish completely its hold on privacy. $28bn was the value of the stock at that time and the 130 partners pulled the float as market conditions (Russian debt crisis plus Long Term Capital Management's calamitous collapse) were against it.

This is *the main risk* for significant stock placements. The market might not take them, there was at that juncture no wriggle room with markets destabilised all around them—east and west, literally.

Another country which is sensitive to stock market conditions, acutely sensitive, is Saudi Arabia. The talk of the town among the wolves of Wall Street has been the imminent floatation and IPO of Aramco, the huge oil conglomerate. Reuters earlier reported that a group of financial advisers had abandoned a plan to sell 5% of the firm. This was the deal; the company planned to hold on to a rather significant 95% stake yet is ultra-sensitive on the market conditions for the remaining 5%. The news agency quoted a source suggesting the decision was taken some time ago but was not being announced.

What does this tell us? Greed affects risk tolerance. The Saudis clearly want every last cent from the public for this floatation. It also tells a story about modern capitalism: "never say low, not high, not die, LOW!"

It may not entirely surprise you to learn that in the worsening market conditions at the time, $7bn was the revised value of the above near $30bn, so it was about getting a far superior price; this again represents in essence, corporate greed.

Goldman Sachs was, and still is to an extent, a little bit "Teflon" though. They successfully got an IPO away in 1999, so after a century and a quarter of being a private partnership this was dissolved, and the firm became publicly owned. The US Treasury bailed out Goldman in 2008 to the tune of just over $10billion as part of Mr Barak Obama's TARP—Troubled Assets Relief Program)[113]. The investment bank, at the time of the disaster in 2007-2008 was running a successful trading arm that was "shorting" the market[114], alongside a "brokerage" arm that was advocating investing in the market over short-, medium- and long-term time frames. There then followed the tale of Mr Paulson who was tempted into the Treasury (in mega-crisis) by the same President Barak Obama. This must have been an expensive deal for all concerned except Hank, of

---

[113] Not sure? All we know from some opaque quotes on Wikipedia is that Goldman Sachs took a $12.9bn bail-out from the US Treasury. Too big to fail again!?

[114] Short selling is the sale of an equity, borrowing it from a holder, then buying it back at a lower price after a market fall.

course, who stashed another nest egg beneath his comfortable cushion.

I think from a risk perspective this has to be viewed sceptically. Paulson was and is an arch elitist; he more than anyone spread the practice of a prolonged period of quantitative easing (the other exponent being then Prime Minister of Great Britain, Gordon Brown). THIS HAS PUMPED ASSET PRICES BACK UP TO UNSUSTAINABLE AND UNREALISTIC LEVELS [115], yet fund managers continue by and large to avoid cash, staying as they say, fully invested. It is not a question of if but when this bubble gently deflates or bursts explosively—more is likely.

Solyndra, June 2010

Solyndra was pulled in 2010 from IPO; once again this was blamed upon "adverse market conditions". The equity appetite had recovered from the 2008 slump but sluggish would still seem to be the right term. Operational and growth strategy, it suddenly announced was going to mostly be funded from the $175m it had just raised (stand-alone) from its existing equity backers. So again elitist and greed were the watchwords.

The $175m had come with a further "capital required" caveat. Yet CEO Chris Gromet was already clearing $400,000 in salary excluding bonuses and share options. It turns out that with growth plans and $175m in place, Solyndra could **not**

---

[115] The practice, it goes without saying was copied by the European Central Bank and Goldman Sachs playing its part by placing large tranches of government debt of the likes of Portugal, Spain, Greece and Italy, all of whose economies were demonstrably unhealthy when compared to Germany, which would finish up footing an enormous bill.

raise the $350m it needed (or rather it saw that it needed at that time).

As the *Wall Street Journal* and *Fortune Magazine* reported at the time, the shareholders' reserves depletion and the negative cash flows put the renewable energy company's future in doubt.

Prada, June 2011

My purpose in exhibiting these IPOs of varying success is to demonstrate to the reader that early strategy which contains a "flip" IPO is often a flawed plan. Phillippe Edmonds, former England cricketer and "oil exploration entrepreneur" has made fortunes arbitraging the financial markets (yes, that includes pension funds) by placing large amounts of bonds and equity and then coming unstuck with the financial model; exploration which involves moving earth and communities is very costly. Edmonds was taking the funding up front and failing to deliver returns. This is just one example; there are more.

Salvatore Ferragamo and Moncler are two of the significant brands of which Prada has control. In their 2011 expansion the businesses required cash in order to expand and grow. Founded back in 1913, the brands it owns today appear in all the high-end fashion magazines and retailers. Hong Kong was a target market and $9bn was its fundraising target back in 2011.

It listed in 2001 in Italy, its host nation. After the demise of the business model, it had to liquidate German brands that it had expensively purchased. By 2011, Miuccia and her husband Patrizio Bertelli still possessed 95% of the equity. So, it clearly still had the challenges and some would say embedded bad practices of the (typically dysfunctional) family business.

In said year, Prada only raised $2.14billion, well short of expectations and much below the anticipated price point.

Kozmo, March-August 2000

Kozmo, at the time of filing for an IPO in 2000, was a popular home delivery service. Founded in 1997 by Joseph Park and Yong Kang, over twenty years ago which was just at the start of the broadband-fed push into internet technologies which opened up a big market in "delivering delivery" i.e. the last mile became (and remains) a huge challenge; Kozmo stepped into the challenge with gusto. By 1999, it had a compound growth rate of 30%. Impressive. In the early days of Amazon, it invested just over $60m into Kozmo. On the *"Money: How Stuff Works"* front page, the company was named as number 4 in the top 10 IPO flops of all time. "Day-glo" delivery vehicles and other stunts, for a smallish business with tiny margins, cost the firm $280million of equity capital. The company axed 24 employees on the same day as announcing that it was pulling the proposed Initial Public Offering. It did at one stage employ over 2,000 people, working across ten cities within the US.

Harrah's/Caesar's Entertainment, October-November 2010

The world's largest casino operator by revenue, like many other growing businesses, their plan was to "build it into growth". It was owned by a private equity company partnership between Apollo and TBG Capital. Paulson and Co was selling in a separate transaction 30.24 million shares. Debt levels at the company would level out at around $19bn and equity of just $2.3bn. At this stage, 9% of the company was worth $500m. That values the company at some $5.555bn which indicates that it was leveraged. On 10 November 2010, the company cancelled the IPO.

Reuters reported in 2010 that Harrah's filed for a much larger $500mn IPO. It changed its name simultaneously to Caesars Entertainment Corporation.

STOP PRESS

2019 (May)—The anciently British, British Steel Corporation PLC was going to prepare itself for administration (bankruptcy). In 1999, Koningkiljke Hoogovens had merged with the distressed British Steel to form and market themselves as Corus PLC. In 2007, in order to stay afloat, the aluminium production units were sold off and the merged entity was bought by Tata Steel of Indian notoriety. The Asians wasted little time in asset-stripping and seeking closure of plants which it claimed were uneconomical, hence the recent announcement in 2019.

On the same day (21/5/2019), Jamie Oliver, a famous UK chef, announced that his chain of restaurants too was stumbling into administration. Oliver put in £30 million of his own cash to try to save the business, but the somewhat befuddled management failed to implement and deliver a salvation plan. I recall in 2010, when I was writing my year 1 doctoral thesis[116], Oliver was braving the tail end of the 2008-2010 recession and opening a Social Enterprise "Fifteen" in the City of London. Staffed by troubled young people, the restaurants thrived, getting lots if young people (back) into work and by the looks of a few of them, actually saving their lives. This was and is what social enterprise must be in this Kingdom, possessing a conscience and relying on young talent.

---

[116] *UK Social Entrepreneurship—The Landscape*

More Lessons From (Elite) Sport

As I concluded this book just prior to the end of a scorching summer, my mind turned to rugby and—to a much lesser extent—football, drawing on my time at Ashridge Business School as part of the faculty (2006-2008) certain key events and themes are emerging in sport that warrant a closer look.

The Two Bs, Bury FC and Bolton Wanderers FC

Both fans and their inherent Supporters' Associations have been maltreated in these two cases. On 28 August 2019, Bury was "ejected" from the football league and this happened overnight; the club had been promising their fans a buyer but everything fell apart.

As Professor Michael Sandel said recently, morality is clearly and blatantly being ignored. As Wimbledon FC did at Milton Keynes two decades ago, things take time; that was agonising for the poor fans (who, after all) paid all the players for their time and toil.

There were emergency meetings taking place at both clubs every other day, yet no clarity or decisions emerged.

Cricket ... again

Then there is the controversial figure of Mr Ben Stokes. In his case I do not see major "risk-related" learnings from his redemption after a night club brawl. What is interesting and necessary in top quality sport is the sheer graft that goes in ... everybody's running the last mile. Stokes is the first man in for training every day; he has Kaizen[1] on the brain in spades.

And—Rugby Union . . . again

Mr Mike Brearley, psychiatry's cricketer, says that Sir Ian Botham only very rarely practiced and Bob Willis England's captain briefly and main strike bowler for a decade, stated that Botham, Gower and Lamb were taking the decisions whilst he was captain. There is a profound lesson here of risk, success, and succession. There MUST be more than one leader on your side if it is to succeed sustainably—winning. Martin Johnson England's skipper in 2003's Rugby Union's World Cup had the following:

Two backs—Matt Dawson and Jonny Wilkinson and
Two forwards- Richard Hill and Laurence Dallaglio.

That's five leaders to take and stay in control of ten others; this is not to mention a certain Jason Leonard on the bench; England's most-ever capped player

BIBLIOGRAPHY

Barclays Bank: Barclays Equity Gilt Study. Published annually courtesy of Courtiers Wealth Management, www.courtiers.co.uk.

Bernstein, Peter L. *FT Mastering Risk Volume 1: Concepts.* Pearson Education Ltd., 2001.

Boyd, R. *Fatal Risk: A Cautionary Tale of AIG's Corporate Suicide.* Wiley Publishing, 2011.

Brearley, J.M. *On Form.* Little Brown Publishing Company, 2017.

Britton, Ronald. *Navigation.* https://ronaldbritton.co.uk/

Casner, Steve. *Careful! The Surprising Science Behind Everyday Calamities—and how you can avoid them.* Pan Macmillan, 2017.

Casner, Steve. *Risk: Why Smart People Have Dumb Accidents.* Pan Macmillan, 2017.

Chomsky, N. *Who Rules the World: Reframings.* Penguin Publishing, 2017.

Dennett, Daniel C. *Bacteria to Bach and Back.* Allen Lane, 2017.

Forster, E.M. *A Passage to India.* Wiley Publications, 1924.

Gardner, D. *Risk: The Science and Politics of Fear.* Virgin Books, 2009.

Godin, S. *The Dip*. Portfolio Publishing, 2007.

Gratton, G. *The Shift—The Future of Work*. Harper Collins Business, 2011.

International Brotherhood of Electrical Workers. "Fixing the Grid's #1 Problem". *The Electrical Worker Online*, July 2019. http://www.ibew.org/articles/19ElectricalWorker/EW1907/index.html

Kasparov, G. *Deep Thinking*. John Murray Publishers, 2017.

Kay, J. *Other People's Money*. Profile Books, Ltd., 2016.

Khanna, P. *The Future is Asian*. Weidenfeld & Nicolson, 2019.

King, M. *The End of Alchemy*. W. W. Norton & Company, Inc., 2016.

Kytle, B. and Ruggie, J.G. *Corporate Social Responsibility as Risk Management*. Harvard University, The John F. Kennedy School of Government, 2005.

Philosophy and Progress. *The Realist* 1.1 April 1929 pp. 64-77.

Piketty, T. and Goldhammer, A. *Capital in the 21st Century*. Éditions du Seuil, 2013.

Rachman, G, *Easternization*, 2018

Rand, Ayn. *Atlas Shrugged*. Penguin Random House, LLC, 2007.

Religion and Philosophy. ISBN 185506 317-4. 1916.

Rorty, R. *Contingency, Irony and Solidarity*. Cambridge University Press, 1989.

Shinar, Y. *Think Like A Winner*. Vermillion, 2007.

Shelp, R. *Fallen Giant: The Amazing Story of Hank Greenberg and the History of AIG*. John Wiley & Sons Inc., 2009.

Sterne, Lawrence. *The Life and Times of Tristram Shandy.* 9 Volumes. Penguin Classics, 1759–1767.

Tett, G. *Fools' Gold.* Little Brown Publishing Co., 2010.

Thaler, R. and Sunstein, C. *Nudge, Improving decisions about Health, Wealth and Happiness.* Caravan Books, 2008.

The Silo Effect: The Peril of Expertise and the Promise of Breaking Down. Little Brown Publishing Co., 2015.

"UK Corporate Governance Code and the Legislative Framework." LawTeacher.net. 11 2013. All Answers Ltd. 09 2019 <https://www.lawteacher.net/free-law-essays/company-law/do-the-uk-corporate-governance-law-essays.php?vref=1>.

Virgil. *The Aeneid.* Publisher Unknown.

Woodward, Sir C. *Winning.* Hodder & Stoughton, 2005.

Woody, Brock. *American Gridlock: Commonsense 101 Solutions to the Economic Crisis. Why the Right and the Left are both Wrong.* H. John Wiley & Sons, Hoboken NJ, 2012.

Wolf, M. *The Shifts and The Shocks—What we've learned and still have to learn from the financial crisis.* Penguin Publishing, 2015.

www.ingramcontent.com/pod-product-compliance
Lightning Source LLC
LaVergne TN
LVHW041635060526
838200LV00040B/1574